D0732489

MYSTERIES OF THE DREAM-TIME

'Cowan's work raises questions and stirs our spiritual consciousness.' W. Lambrecht, *Parabola*

'James Cowan brings with him quite another kind of understanding.' Kathleen Raine, *Resurgence*

MYSTERIES OF
THE DREAM-TIME

THE SPIRITUAL LIFE
OF AUSTRALIAN ABORIGINES

JAMES COWAN

Revised edition

PRISM · UNITY

First published in Great Britain in 1989 and reprinted 1990. This
new edition published 1992 by
PRISM PRESS
2 South Street,
Bridport,
Dorset DT6 3NQ

Distributed in the USA by
ATRIUM PUBLISHERS GROUP
3356 Coffey Lane,
Santa Rosa, CA 95403

Published in Australia by
UNITY PRESS,
P.O. Box 532,
Woollahra,
NSW 2025

1 85327 077 6

Printed and bound in the Channel Islands
by The Guernsey Press Company Limited.

Contents

For
Richard Dickinson
frater

Photographs

1. A view from one of the caves in Obiri Rock, Arnhemland Escarpment area. Many of these caves have been overpainted by successive generations since the first inhabitants arrived over the land bridge from Asia, 50,000 years ago. Obiri Rock, like Nourlangie and Uluru (Ayers Rock), is an 'Open-air Cathedral' recording the sacred images of the Aboriginal culture.

2. Lightning Man, Nourlangie Rock. Note the tiny axeheads protruding from his body and limbs. These, clashing against the heavens, create lightning during the rainy season, a pontifical statement nevertheless from the Dreaming.

3. Lightning Man, Namargin, painted in the X-ray style unique to this region of Australia. His 'inner' body is revealed in its physiological exactitude as well as a patterned work of art.

4. Barramundie fish and Spirit Figures, Nourlangie Rock. Without facial expression, these Spirit Figures are iconic representations of spirit types rather than individual people.

5. Male tribesman painted in the 'stick' style, an earlier style to that of X-ray. He is carrying hunting equipment such as spears and a stone axe, as well as dilly bags.

6. Part of the main freize, Nourlangie Rock, depicting a confrontation between Lightning Man and his wife (*top figure*) and Namanjolk, a malign Spirit Figure. This frieze was retouched by Barramundie Charlie some 20 years ago. Since then he has died. It is unlikely that any of his friends have the technical expertise to renew this remarkable painting. Unfortunately, ritual renewal by surviving members of the tribe has so far failed to re-occur. If this situation should continue, then the *djang* of this important hot place will eventually diminish.

7. Barramundie fish and female Spirit Figure painted in the X-ray style, Nourlangie Rock.

8. Sea turtle painted in the X-ray style. Turtles are speared in the ocean off the coast of Arnhemland.

Photographs by Colin Beard

Introduction

In the past, the spirituality of the Australian Aborigines has often been characterized as a collection of superstitions and primitive myths that were deemed incapable of supporting a genuine religious life. For two centuries observers have been looking at Aboriginal beliefs anthropologically in order to detach them from their roots in the culture itself. This has led to a subsequent diminution of the flame among Aborigines themselves. Messianic Christianity in the form of well-intentioned missionaries sought to undermine Aboriginal spirituality even further in the belief that Aborigines had been 'living in darkness' prior to the advent of Jesus Christ in their lives.

As a result, the Aborigines found themselves the victims of cultural genocide. Not only were they destroyed physically as a race, but they looked on with impotence as their traditions, their way of life and their beliefs were swept aside. Without treaties to protect them, without even official acknowledgement of their humanity (as late as the 1950s Aborigines had few civil rights under the law), they were left to live out their lives on the fringe of European settlement — a disenfranchised race of nomads doomed to extinction. It was assumed by many that they had no will to live anyway, since they had taken to self-abuse by way of alcohol and disease. Indeed, the twilight of their existence as a race was seen as a necessary but rather unfortunate transition. When Aboriginal poet, Kath Walker, wrote her book, 'We Are Going', during the 1960s, it aroused little interest among administrators, and was assessed from a literary rather than a cultural standpoint.

Thus an exquisite jewel was about to be erased from the face of the earth. That spiritual abode known as the Dreaming was about to be pulled down in favour of a new edifice built around the idea of assimilation, European-style housing projects and the incursion of geologists preaching mineral wellbeing. The Aborigines, moreover, were given little say in

1

their fast diminishing destiny. They were asked instead to give up their old ways, cease their nomadism, relinquish their totems and learn to adjust to the emptiness of a material existence foisted upon them from outside.

Yet the strength of this remarkably resilient race rests in their refusal to lie down and die, in their refusal to give up the old ways. In the early days they resisted the European invaders by force; in more recent times they have become politicized. Today, Land Rights is the banner under which they wage war against indifference and apathy. They want to survive, if only because they still believe in the power of the Dreaming as a way of life. The mystical tradition so profoundly linked to the events of the Dreaming is an important bulwark for them against the threat of extinction.

This book endeavours to focus attention on little-known aspects of the Dreaming. I have not attempted to explore in great detail the diversity of myths, nor the variety of ritual practices that individual tribes might regard as their spiritual heritage. This is not the place to do so. Instead I have tried to highlight the similarities that exist with other great religious traditions so that the Dreaming can be seen for what it is: the metaphysical expression of primordial truths that trace the birth of the world and man's place in it. I have tried to show that the Dreaming is not an alien place populated by unrecognizable spirit-beings, but a place of metaphysical repose for the Aborigine.

The Dreaming, moreover, is a fragile place. It remains to be seen whether it will open its gates to a world increasingly inured to the idea of 'enchantment' as a prefiguration of grace. For it to weave its spell again, men and women of all creeds and beliefs will need to throw off the cloak of logic and ratiocination, and accept the mytho-poetry of the Dreaming as a supernatural reality. They will have to recognize also that the Aborigines have made the 'face of the earth' their Bhagavad Gita, their Torah, their Bible or Koran. Indeed the Dreaming is the Aboriginal Ark of the Covenant which they have been carrying about the

Australian continent since the beginning of time.

During the course of researching this book I was fortunate enough to meet with a number of knowledgeable Aborigines — men such as Toby Gangale of the Mirarr Kuwjai:mi tribe, Big Bill Neidjie of the Bunidji tribe, and Idumdum of the Wardaman tribe in Northern Australia. These men and others spoke to me in detail about the metaphysical aspects of their culture. In doing so, they allowed me to enter into their world and partake of certain experiences that contributed to a deeper understanding on my part of Aboriginal spirituality. I must emphasize, however, that I did not undergo any tribal initiation ceremony, nor did I feel this was necessary. Instead we shared the excitement of discovering areas of commonality derived from our respective traditions and beliefs; areas that served to bind rather than separate us as human beings.

Indeed, more than anything, I learnt to respect the Aboriginal people for their essential humanity. So often did I encounter the uncluttered wisdom of their thought that I began to marvel at their ability to derive so much spiritual knowledge from what appeared, on the surface, to be an uncritical respect for tradition. I soon learnt to understand that the source of their inner knowledge was not an uncritical respect but reverence. For Aborigines, the numen is embodied in all things manifest. This in turn yields a concept of sanctity more complex, and more far-reaching than any that we might find in the universal religions.

At the same time, my Aboriginal friends taught me a great deal that was immediatley practical in terms of my own life. They taught me how to respect and understand landscape. They taught me the importance of ritual. And they taught me to value the initiatory process as a means of realizing inner knowledge. I am grateful to them for simplifying my ideals in a way that made gnosis possible.

What I recall most about my journeys among these people, whether they were among tribesmen of the North, or among those I met in the North-west of Australia, or among the fringe-dwellers around outback towns in New South Wales, was their willingness to communicate metaphysical realities. I gained the impression that Aborigines are a unique race because they are utterly possessed by the Dreaming. The Dreaming means more to them than political or social issues because it is the only unsullied possession left to them. Everything else has been taken from them; thus they have been forced to make a choice between travelling down two forks in the road: that of assimilation and cultural oblivion, or re-affirmation of the Dreaming as a metaphysical reality and the long road back to re-discovering their cultural identity.

Nights spent in the open under starscapes pregnant with hiero-figures from the Dreaming; days spent wandering along spiritual paths through the landscape; hours spent in caves under the watchful gaze of Spirit-beings — so many experiences have gone into the making of this book. It has been a gift of the Aboriginal people, both past and present. Hopefully any new insights of mine gained during the course of my wanderings may help to clarify their world of the Dreaming for others.

Some of these chapters have appeared in journals such as *Temenos, Studies in Comparative Religion, Connaissances des Religions, Avaloka* and *Parabola*. I would like to thank my friend, Dr Kathleen Raine, for her encouragement and to all those Aboriginal friends who have enlightened me over the years. Their wit and humanity, their sagacity and complete lack of bitterness have made it possible for mutual respect and understanding to grow up between us. I only hope that I have been able to render with some degree of veracity the extraordinary luminosity of their spiritual world for others to enter as I have done.

J.C.
Sydney, 1988

CHAPTER 1
Spiritual Discipline and Psychic Power

In any living tradition there must always be cultural exemplars who reflect a condition of primordiality which acts as a link between the natural and supernatural worlds. Such men (and occasionally women) possess certain qualities of behaviour and, more properly, a presence that others may recognize as being distinctively different. Among indigenous cultures such as Aborigines or American Indians these cultural exemplars are men who have undergone a ritual initiation that sets them apart from other members of their tribe. Yet this initiatory activity is separate from those rituals normally associated with the passage from adolescence into manhood. In the context of Aboriginal society the making of a *karadji*,[1] or clever man, is a vocation like any other spiritual discipline; few men are called to it and even fewer survive the psychic terrors that are so often inherent in its attainment.

To a great extent the words 'clever man', 'sorcerer' or 'medicine man' are 19th century pejorative expressions designed to demean the role of the *karadji* within the context of Aboriginal society. He was looked upon by many observers, including a number who were ostensibly sympathetic to the Aborigines, as at best an eccentric figure capable of beneficent acts of medicine; and at worst, a trickster or charlatan. This opinion lingered on for a long time into the 20th century, so that the *karadji* himself soon found his position within his tribe undermined by the community's encounter with modern medicine, the Church missionary system and the corrupting influence of its own society living under the threat of extinction. His importance as the guardian of traditional culture and sacred lore was progressively eroded by contact with European civilization to the point where he was regarded as no more than an imposter and tribal scamp. One reputable observer even went so far as to suggest that the doctors 'were the greatest swindlers and conjurers, who, by means of their deceits and frauds were able to keep the people in dependance upon them'[2].

Such a view made it virtually impossible for the genuine *karadji* to maintain his honoured position within Aboriginal society. Following his demise, the way was open for white authorities (whether administrative or in the guise of Church missionary zeal) to undermine the cultural and religious stability of Aboriginal society altogether by supplanting the visionary imperatives established by the *karadji* with a more prosaic 'Christian' ethic designed to encourage Aboriginal assimilation. It was a policy of cultural genocide that has in consequence all but wiped out traditional Aboriginal life in Australia.

But what was it about the person of the *karadji* that so threatened the invading white culture? Why was it so necessary to discredit him as a living embodiment of other-worldy experience? It is a question that we wish to address in the course of discovering how these clever men received their vocation, and from there attained to the highest levels of spiritual knowledge and discipline to which they espoused. For it is only in the context of this classic confrontation between Western materialism, in all its various guises, and the traditional *karadji* in his role as a cultural and metaphysical exemplar, that we begin to perceive the dilemma that faces any traditional society in its fight for survival. What happened yesterday among Aborigines with the destruction of their spiritual and mythological heritage is an event that continues to occur in many parts of the world even today.

The prefix 'clever' appertaining to a *karadji* means much more than adroitness, neat in movement, skillful or dexterous. Probably it was the nearest equivalent English word to equate with that of the indiginous language, although it fails to convey fully the intellectual qualification required in order to become a *karadji*. Perhaps its other aspect of 'seizing what is imperceptible' might come nearer to a description of the *karadji*'s inherent ability to bridge the gap between what is manifested and the spirit-world of the Dreaming. In any event, the implication of acute intelligence combined with a readiness to associate with older *karadji* during his youth were what distinguished a potential postulant from his contemporaries. In some cases this difference was recognized to be physical as well. Berndt[3] actually suggests that a postulant is noticably different from other young boys by 'the light radiating from his eyes'. This would accord with the idea of a light dwelling within the 'square inch' or in the 'face' as depicted in the Bardo Thodal, or Tibetan Book of the Dead[4].

More often than not a father would initiate his son into the role of *karadji*. Thus the concept of a spiritual patronomy being handed on from father to son was an important part of acquiring a vocation. In some cases a postulant was actually called a *walamiradalmai* or 'one to whom cleverness has been handed on'. However, the power associated with becoming a *karadji* was not something that a father could bestow upon his son. Such power could only be acquired from the great Baiami (All-father) himself. In other words, while the father or an older *Karadji* may have the right to educate a postulant to full clever man status, they could only do so on the understanding that the postulant had already been made aware of his vocation, often through visionary contact with his Dreaming ancestors. Only when the father or the older *Karadji* has been advised by Baiami in a dream that the postulant was ready did the full process of initiation begin.

Circumstantial and oral testimony suggest that the would-be *karadji* underwent a complex form of initiation that involved both ritual 'death' at the hands of *karadji* or *Oruncha* (Spirits), accompanied by prolonged bouts of meditation in the wilderness. The ritual killing as an act varied in detail throughout Australia, although the principal motifs remained the same. Among the Arunta of the Central Desert region, the officiants extract small clear crystals from their bodies which they proceeded to press slowly and strongly along the front of the postulant's legs up to his breastbone. As they did so, the skin was scored at intervals in order to facilitate entry of the crystals into the postulant's body. The postulant then lay down while the officiants jerked their hands towards him, all the while holding other crystals. Scoring was repeated and more crystals rubbed into the postulant's scalp. Meanwhile, a hole was cut under the first finger of the right hand and a crystal inserted. Finally, the postulant was asked to eat meat and drink water into which a small amount of crystals had been placed. This rite was then repeated on the second and third days, after which a large hole was cut in his tongue as a sign that the power has entered him. Grease was then rubbed all over his body and a sacred representation of the *Oruncha* painted on his chest — symbol of the Spirit-men (Sky Heroes) who have made him a *karadji*. Fur string and gum nuts were placed upon his head in ritual adornment. He was then told that he must remain at the men's camp until his wounds had healed. As well, he was to observe certain food taboos, sleep with a fire between himself and his wife as a sign to the *Oruncha*, and hold himself aloof from everyone. Otherwise the power that had entered his body on initiation may leave him altogether[5].

This was only one method. Another way required the postulant to sleep at the mouth of a cave and await the visit of an *Oruncha* at daybreak. The spirit threw an invisible spear which pierced the postulant's neck from behind and passed through his tongue, making the ritual hole to signify the receipt of the power. A second spear passed through the head from ear to ear. The posulant fell down dead at this point and is carried into the depths of the cave. Here the spirit removed the victim's internal organs and replaced them with a new set, along with quartz crystal on which his power ultimately depended. (The parallels here with Egyptian mummification practices are obvious in the way that the body is prepared for its new life after ritual 'death'). When the man eventually came to life again he experienced a period of insanity. Only when he partly recovered did the

Oruncha lead him back to his own people who then decorated his nose with a band of powdered charcoal as a sign of his partial entry into the Order.

Thus ends the first phase of the making of a *karadji*. Under normal circumstances, the postulant was not allowed to perform any *karadji* functions for a full year, otherwise the power that had entered him through the insertion of quartz crystals would desert him. It did not mean however that his education had been completed, for in many way the most important period of a *karadji*'s transition into the other-worldly aspects of his profession had only just begun. Finer details in the art of bone-pointing, sorcery, diagnostic techniques in the cure of illness and psychic healing were all taught to the novice *karadji* by his elders during this period. These were the more practical aspects of the *karadji*'s professional expertise and underlay the important social contribution that the man made to his community in the role of doctor. Yet they do not convey fully the spiritual metamorphosis that the man had undergone in his pursuit of the power associated with the ritual insertion of the quartz crystals — and indeed the death and rebirth that he had undergone at the hands of the *Oruncha*, or the tribal officiants.

Here we must look more closely at the use of such artifacts as stones, bones, australites and particularly quartz crystals as power-bearers of rich symbolic significance. To an east coast tribe these quartz crystals were known as 'wild stones' and were said to embody the Great Spirit himself[6]. The use of quartz crystal as an iconic representation of Baiami has its parallels in other cultures as well. The Taoists, for example, regarded jade as a medicine of similar import. In one alchemical text of the 4th century A.D. jade was regarded as a *hsien* medicine and 'the life of those who take *hsuan-chen* (Mysterious Truth, an alias for jade) is without end . . . . Jade powder, if taken alone or with water, confers immortality . . . . It causes the eater to fly up to be a hsien in heaven'[7]. Eliade goes so far as to suggest that the quartz crystal owes its extraordinary prestige to its celestial origin, as originally Baiami's throne was made of crystal. In other words, these crystals are supposed to have fallen to earth from heaven as 'solidified light'[8ab]. The Sea Dayaks too considered quartz crystals as 'light stones', regarding this solidified light as being of a supernatural origin. However much one might wish to explore the light symbolism of quartz crystals as a scintilla of divine attributes, it becomes obvious that their insertion into a postulant represents a significant step in the process of deification of the individual concerned. He dies and is 'reborn' on the third day as a spiritual being capable of performing feats of magic and healing at one and the same time. In Mowaldjali's testament[9] on the making of a *karadji* the importance of quartz crystals as sacred objects is explicit. He says that the bodies of the magicians overflow with magic stones called *gedji*. With these inside them they can see vast distances and into other realms. In particular they are able to see into the underworld and observe the spirits-of-the-dead all bunched together there.

Accompanying this transformation, postulants were often seen to grow feathers on their arms which, after a few days, developed into wings. Taoists also believe that when a man obtains the *tao* feathers begin to grow on his body. Plato made the same suggestion in Phaedrus (249e) when he wrote, 'A man beholds the beauty of the world, is reminded of truth and beauty, and his wings begin to grow'. In the *Pancavimca Brahmana.* (IV. 1,13) the symbolic explanation is even more explicit when it states that 'he who understands has wings'. The use of feathers, then, as an expression of spiritual transformation is widely documented. In the context of the making of a *karadji* this practice quite obviously signifies an important moment in his transition from being an ordinary tribal member to that of a 'man of high degree'.

Acquiring a new name signifying the rebirth of the individual concerned exemplifies this transition[10]. Although the neophyte has become a member of the Order of *karadji* and is already capable of a number of magical tricks that serve to re-affirm the presence of the quartz crystal-derived power in his person, these are only a small part of his professional armory.

Their significance is exoteric insofar as a *karadji* must be seen to occupy a socially contributive position within his community as well. If he is not healing sickness, curing mental disorders, exorcising demons or assessing the identity of murderers in the context of the normal process of dying, then he is involved in developing his own mediumistic powers through long sojourns in the wilderness and prolonged bouts of meditation.

In this respect a great deal of emphasis is placed upon breathing techniques among *karadji*, similar to those used in hesychastism[11]. One reports suggests that a *karadji* used to sit on the bottom of a river for days at a time, talking with a spirit known as Konikatine. He was able to hold his breath for the entire period of his immersion, returning to the surface with bloodshot eyes and covered in ooze[12]. This concurs with an experience related by Pao-P'u-Tzu when he spoke of his great uncle Hsien-kung who, when very drunk one hot summer day, 'would go to the bottom of a deep pool and stay there for almost a day, because he was able to keep the *ch'i* (ethereal essence) and to breathe like an embryo'. Such claims may not be factual in a physiological sense (although it would be a risk to discount them entirely), they do indicate a pre-occupation with meditational breathing techniques among *karadji* similar to those practised in other spiritual disciplines.

In fact one is constantly struck by the similarities that exist between the Taoist *hsien* and the Aboriginal *karadji*. Both have subsidiary roles to play as resident diagnosticians within their respective communities. Both engage in magical acts such as prolonged flight[13]. Both are said to turn lighter in body colour on the assumption of their position of *karadji* or *hsien*. And both express themselves in a complex symbolic language and ritual action that is in part animistic. While for the *hsien* there is the alchemical association culminating in a desire to produce gold or the attainment of immortality, these disciplines find their paradigm in the *karadji*'s desire to develop his 'inner eye' or powers of spiritual discernment to the point where he becomes an 'expert'.

Possessing the 'inner eye' of course has numerous practical applications. In his role as tribal doctor, the *karadji* is often called upon to use his inner eye in diagnosing internal ailments. Mowaldjali, in his testimony, gives a clear outline of the functional use of the inner eye. 'The diagnostician's eye, that is the magic eye, is the one which he checks the liver, the urine, the gall-bladder, the heart and the intestines. He checks these completely. "Ah yes," he says, (ie. the *karadji*) "the trouble is in the back of the neck!" He *sees* (our italics) perfectly . . . they call him the expert. He is trained by the *rai* (spirits/*Oruncha*). In the beginning, he is unable to see very far. His sight is still dim. As yet he doesn't know (understand). So the *rai*, they send a spirit animal or insect out to him. Then his eyes begin to open and he is astonished. That's the way he begins to see further and further. "Did you see far?" he is asked. "I saw the *rai*," he replied. "Ah, very good. You are getting better and better. You are becoming an expert at seeing these animals and insects. (ie. the *rai*)" '.

We are confronted here with an angelic disposition. It is said that the *rai* are those spirits that are responsible for teaching *karadji* the esoteric aspects of his profession. At the same time, differentiation is made between the inner eye and the use of ordinary eyes for normal perception. "*We* think he is looking with his ordinary eyes," Mowaljali suggests. But really the *karadji* is observing with his inner eye, a gift of the *rai*. In this respect one would hesitate to ask whether so-called 'X-ray' paintings popular among Northern Territory tribes are a formalization of the capacity for inner eye observation. Empirical knowledge would of course provide the information and images for these paintings to be made. But this does not explain why the painters would wish to depict the internal organs as if they were being observed from outside the body. Perhaps the *karadji*'s ability to see within with his inner eye provided the initial inspiration for this style of painting.

The inner eye has other applications which reach beyond those of a purely diagnostic character. Through the use of the inner eye as a meditative device, the *karadji* is able to make contact with the spirit-realm and its inhabitants, the *rai*. In this respect Berndt's free translation of a text related to him by a Yaralde tribesman stresses the importance that *karadji* place upon meditation as a mode of contact between themselves and the spirit-world.

'When you see an old man sitting by himself over there in the camp, do not disturb him, for if you do he will "growl" at you. Do not play near him, because he is sitting down by himself with his thoughts in order *to see*. He is gathering those thoughts so that he can feel and hear. Perhaps he then lies down, *getting into a special posture*, so that he can *see* while sleeping [ie. meditating]. He sees indistinct visions and hears 'persons' [*rai/ Oruncha*] talk in them. He gets up and looks for those he has *seen*, but not seeing them, he lies down again in the prescribed manner, so as to see what he has *seen* before. He puts his head on the pillow as previously so as to *see* [ie. invoke a vision] as before. Getting up, he tells his friends to strengthen that power [known as *miwi*], a constituent of the quartz crystals within themselves, so that when they lie down they will be able to see and feel (or become aware of) people present, and in that way they will perceive them.'

Not surprisingly, this *miwi* or 'power' is said to be present in all persons, though especially developed only by a few. It is said to be located in the pit of the stomach, which must be considered as a generalized symbolic location similar to the base of the spine as referred to in Kundalini yoga. According to Hindu tradition, *kundalini* which is a form of *shakti*, is always considered to be present in the human being and is represented by a coiled-up snake. Like the *luz* bone also, that indestructible kernel said to contain those elements necessary for the restoration of an individual being under the influence of 'celestial dew' (one cannot help noticing the physical similarity here between celestial dew and the solidified light of quartz crystals as a power-bearer), the *kundalini* snake can be taught to rise up through the various plexuses in order to reach the 'third eye'. In other words, the *luz/miwi/kundalini* nexus, when developed, can precipitate a restoration of the primordial state and so bring about man's recovery of his sense of eternity[14].

If this is so, then we are close to identifying the essential nature of the *miwi* power so closely associated with quartz crystals. For snakes figure largely in the *karadji* initiation ceremonies throughout Australia and are closely associated with the presence of these wild stones. In one case a postulant is taken up to heaven, either on a cord or a rainbow which serves as a rope. There he is 'killed' and impregnated with quartz crystals as well as tiny rainbow snakes. In another ceremony, a postulant is shown a tiger-snake which leads him into a hole full of snakes that made him clever by rubbing themselves against him. Daisy Bates claimed that a *karadji* she once met had the power to hold communion with a mythical snake named Kajoora. In each case we are looking at some sort of spiritual realization accompanying the symbolic presence of snakes in one way or another. It is important to note that even if snakes are physically present on occasions during these ceremonies, their function is largely symbolic. Like *kundalini* serpent-power, they are capable of communing with the inner eye of a *karadji* and so release *miwi*, or power.

Of course, this is not without its dangers. As in any intense spiritual discipline psychic terrors are always lurking, ready to play havoc with the postulant's mental stability. Our Yaralde tribesman vividly reminds us of the psychic risks a postulant runs in becoming a *karadji*: 'When you sit down to see the prescribed visions, and you see them, do not be frightened, because they will be horrible. They are hard to describe, though they are in my mind and my *miwi*, and though I could project the experience into you after you have been well trained.

'However, some of them are evil spirits. Some are like snakes, some are like horses with men's heads [centaurs?], and some are spirits of evil men which resemble burning fires. You see your camp burning and the floodwaters rising, and thunder, lightning and rain, the earth rocking, the earth moving, the hills moving, the water whirling, and the trees which still stand, swaying about. Do not be frightened. If you get up you will not see these scenes, but when you lie down again you will see them, unless you get too frightened. If you do you will break the web (or thread) on which the scenes are hung. You may see dead persons walking towards you, and you will hear their bones rattle. If you hear and see these things without fear, you will never be frightened of anything. These dead people will not show themselves to you again, because your *miwi* is now strong. You are now powerful because you have seen these dead people.'

Here we see the *miwi* power addressed as a separate entity to the intellectual energy of the *karadji*. It too is capable of being affected by untoward visionary experience, yet at the same time able to develop a psychic power of its own. This would accord with any bona fide meditational technique designed to release dormant psychic or spiritual energy so that it rises in phases to the 'crown of the head'. What this Yaralde tribesman is speaking of is the effective conquest of the higher states of being within himself. The process of disintegration, of arresting manifestation, is the one sure way of finding the primordial, motionless unity that existed before the rupture between himself and the spirit realm of the Dreaming.

Much emphasis is placed upon displays of magic and extraordinary events by *karadji*, such as climbing into the sky on aerial ropes, telepathy, speaking in languages, observing monsters, acts of sorcery and bone-pointing in order to justify the title of clever men in the eyes of ethnologists and writers on comparative religion. Unfortunately, little attempt has been made so far to explore the rich symbolic and metaphysical significance of these acts in the light of a viable spiritual discipline. This has lead to a subsequent diminishment of the importance of the *karadji*'s role within Aboriginal society. To equate his visionary experience with other shamanic disciplines again tends to reduce the significance of his spiritual endeavours in a way that identifies them too closely with induced ecstatic experience. What is missing in these studies is a systematic reasoning into why such people embark upon these supernatural or revelatory journeys in the first place. Is this because current thinking has dichotomized the relationship between spiritual and physical wellbeing? One suspects this to be the case. As with most indiginous peoples, their spiritual life, because it is largely oral and esoterically based, has long ago been categorized as being no more than a reflection of so-called 'primitive' mentality. Indeed it is one of the principal foundations of modern philosophy and psychology to suggest that all religious disciplines evolve somehow from archaic models. Thus the spiritual life of Aborigines has always been regarded as undeveloped, and the people themselves as the 'oldest' form of humanity! It is a condition under which Aborigines continue to live today, their lives still an object of anthropological interest separate from any recognition that their culture might be a substantial source of arcane lore and wisdom from which all of us might derive benefit. Until attitudes change profoundly this situation will remain as it is — a more or less tacit acceptance that Aborigines and their way of life represents a monumental cultural impasse in the history of humanity.

The *karadji*, as cultural exemplar, reflected a unique human type. In an inherently conservative society perhaps too much pre-occupied with ancestral allegiance and the past, he often represented a potent force for change. Because of his direct contact with the Dreaming and its pantheon of spirit-figures, he was one of the few people able to create new dances, songs and stories. Through him a tribal community could remain culturally vital and grow accordingly. Although his role sometimes required him to be spiritually oppressive in terms of instilling fear among those who did not fully understand his other-worldly activities, this is not to say that his presence within the tribe was of a negative character. Much of that fear was a mixture of awe and respect anyway. After all, he was different; he had subjected himself to an encounter with Sky Heroes; he had died and been reborn again as a man of 'high degree' with the responsibility to obey both natural and supernatural law. Such experience inevitably set him apart from other men, although he ostensibly lived a normal life within the tribe.

The importance of the *karadji* as resident tribal sage and seer cannot be underestimated. The arcane information at his disposal was a constant source of spiritual security among other tribal members who looked to him for answers in times of uncertainty. He was the only man allowed to have (indeed capable of) contact with Baiami, the All-Father and culture-giver, through the medium of his spirit-messengers, the *Oruncha*. In the tradition of the prophet or seer, he alone had the power to intercede with these Sky Heroes on behalf of his fellow tribesmen. One story relates how a *Karadji* made contact with Baiami in order to request his help in ending a drought afflicting his tribal country. To do this, the *karadji* had to ascend the mountain Oobi-Oobi, beyond the top of which lay Baiami's quartz crystal throne. Coming to the mountain, he discovered footholes cut in the rock in the form of a ladder. He proceeded to climb this ladder for four days until he had reached the top. Here he discovered a stone excavation, into which bubbled up a fresh spring of water. Thirsty after his long climb the *karadji* drank his fill, only to realize how invigorated he now felt. His fatigue had fallen away. Near the spring he noticed a number of circles built from piled up stones, one of which he entered. Immediately he heard the sound of a *gayandi* (bullroarer), the traditional medium through which the voice of Baiami's spirit-messenger communicated with men. Having pleaded his case for the cessation of the drought with them, the *karadji* was raised by some of the attendant *Oranchi* off the sacred mountain of Oobi-Oobi into the numinous presence of Baiami, seated on his crystal throne. Here he was told to gather all the flower blossoms he could carry and convey them back to his tribe. This he did and, with the aid of the *Oranchi*, was transported back to Oobi-Oobi from where he returned to his tribe[15].

This legend, divested of its narrative connotations, is a

17

perfect example of the symbolic mode of thought associated with spiritual transformation that we find at work within Aboriginal cosmology. Here we encounter the remnants of a sacred map as well as a method of approach to the epiphanic state. The 'ladder' that must be climbed reflects the various stages of spiritual development that a *karadji* must undergo on his spiritual journey. Drinking from the 'spring' at the source is inevitably rejuvenating and can only be done after the long and difficult climb has been completed. The *karadji*'s recognition of the sacred mandalas and his 'entry' into one of them (probably each one, although it is not stated) is a universal image of contemplation and spiritual renewal. Of course entry into one of these will precipitate contact with the realm of the Spirit through the medium of 'voices'. At this point the *karadji* finds himself 'raised' by the angelic orders into the very heart of that rarified spiritual realm of Baiami, the All-Father as symbolized by the crystal throne[16]. Not only is it made clear to him here that the 'drought' can be ended through contact with the Dreaming, but only through a distribution of Baiami's 'blossoms' among those living in the physical world can this be truly achieved on a much broader plane. In other words, a *conjunctio* between the supernatural and the natural worlds must by achieved be way of ritual contact and meditation if man's existence on earth is to remain vital.

Such a legend has all the elements found in a sacred text associated with a more literal spiritual discipline. Because it is couched in symbolic language, however, this in no way diminishes its metaphysical significance, nor suggests a lack of sophistication in its method. The *karadji*'s whole being is directed towards intercession on behalf of his people, and of himself. This cannot be achieved through the ratiocinative process solely. Only the symbolic mode of expression can embrace effectively the essentially disparate elements that make up knowledge of the epiphanic state. In this respect, nearly all Aboriginal secret-sacred legends (that is, esoteric) are concerned with the deliniation of metaphysical elements.

Finally one is confronted with the special sanctity embodied in a practising *karadji*. Both his shadow and the 'crown of his head' are considered to be so closely identified with his *miwi* power that it is forbidden (taboo) to touch either of them. To do so is regarded as a sacrilege, and in consequence the crime demands an appropriate form of punishment. Unfortunately, the sacrilege perpetrated upon the *karadji* by European civilization during the past 200 years has continued to go unpunished. In fact, his presence within the tribal community has always been regarded as subversive, precisely because he stood for a dimension of spiritual experience unattainable to those in question. It takes very little to see why outback graziers, colonial authorities and later, government administrators, sought to neutralize his influence within his tribe as far as possible. Squatters had him driven from the land or executed; missionaries and teachers made every attempt to undermine his spiritual authority through the introduction of alien beliefs; doctors brought into ridicule his use of traditional remedies by the flagrant use of modern medicinal techniques; observers and, more latterly, anthropologists emphasised the sorcery aspects of his profession to the detriment of his spiritual attainments. In the end, traditional Aboriginal society was effectively destroyed when the *karadji*, as a cultural exemplar, was considered to be redundant. His *miwi* power flowed from him and was eventually lost. The spiritual knowledge and the ascetic disciplines that needed to be practiced for its attainment have now all but been eradicated. What was left were the remnants of a traditional society trying desperatly to make sense of a world that only he had the power to understand.

If that society is ever to renew itself in the face of Western secular materialism, then his role within the Aboriginal community must be revived. He alone holds the key to renewed contact with the Dreaming and an understanding of the epiphanic state. Without a revival of this knowledge there is no prospect of a continuation of the traditional life of Aborigines in Australia as it once was. C.P. Mountford inadvertantly mourned

19

their loss to the world when he observed 'Day after day I watched the beautiful unclothed bodies of the men as they strode along beside us. They were a continued delight to the eye, their skin shining with health, their rippling muscles and the royal carriage . . .. It is small wonder, then, that the elders should possess a mental poise and balance which belongs only to the best in our civilization'.

Such an epitaph, poignantly expressed as it is, cannot compensate for the disappearance of those 'wild stones', nor the wealth of visionary experience, wisdom and arcane knowledge that went with them, from the spiritual landscape of men's minds. It remains to be seen whether white Australians have the understanding, or indeed desire, to allow such a renascence to occur without destroying it at its inception.

Notes

1. The name of such clever men varies in accordance with the different regions of Australia from where they originate. *Karajji* (Western Districts of New South Wales), *wingirin* (Queensland), *kuldukke* (south of the Murray, Victoria) et al.

2. C. Strehlow. *Die Aranda-und-Loritja-Stamme*, Part 4, p.42.

3. R.M. &C.H. Berndt, *The World of the First Australians*, p.308.

4. Goethe also speaks of the 'eye which itself is the light' in his *Doctrine of Colours (Farmenlehre)* as a method of physiological visionary perception. It is also interesting to note that the traditional Taoist *hsien* postulant could only be detected by his peculiar appearance.

5. Spencer and Gillen, *Native Tribes*. Also A.P. Elkin, *Aboriginal Men of High Degree*.

6. A.C. McDougall, Manners, Customs and Legends of the Coombangree Tribe, *Science of Man* 3:117.

7. Pao-P'u-Tzu, *The Inner Chapters*, transl. by Tenney L. Davis and Ch'en Kuo-fu, American Academy of Arts and Sciences, Vol.74, No.10, Dec. 1941.

8. (a) Mircea Eliade, *The Two and the One*, p. 25. (b) cf. Ezra Pound, *The Cantos*, No. 94 in which he echoes the contemplative writings of Richard of St Victor:

> 'Above prana, the light,
>> past light, the crystal.
> Above crystal, the jade!'

9. H.H. J. Coates, *The Rai and the Third Eye*, Oceana, XXXVII. 1966.

10. Cf. 'Except a man be born again, he cannot see the Kingdom of God'. John 3:3.

11. Cf. Gregory Palamas' remarks: 'Hesychia is the standing still of the mind and of the world, forgetfulness of what is below, initiation into secret knowledge of what is above, the putting aside of thoughts for what is better than they; this is the true activity, the ascent to the true contemplation and vision of God'.

12. P. Beveridge, *The Aborigines of Victoria and the Riverina*, 1889.

13. 'Operators in *thumi* sorcery walk on air which the spirits have made soft and solid for a foot above the earth. The air also moves, carrying the operators direct to their victim. Billy Emu, a famous Weilwan *karadji*, was able to cover 122kms a day, as fast as a horseman', Elkin field notes, 1944. In contrast, Pao-P'u-Tzu maintains that certain *hsien* were capable of travelling 12000 li (about 4000 miles) in one day!

14. René Guenon, *The Lord of the World*.

15. K.L. Parker, *More Australian Legendary Tales*. London 1898.

16. cf. *The Book of Enoch*. 'They elevated me aloft to heaven. I proceeded, until I arrived at a wall built with stones of crystal . . . Attentively I surveyed it, and saw that it contained an exalted throne, the appearance of which was like that of frost.' Chapter XIV.

CHAPTER 2
Landscape as Tradition and Metaphor

'The whole countryside is his living, age-old family tree.'
T.G. Strehlow

It has been said that landscapes such as those that existed in places like Australia prior to European contact in the 18th and 19th centuries were utterly pristine. That is, they did not embody any signs of culture, let alone a sacred one, since there was no visible 'proof' in the form of man-made structures or indeed examples of any formal artistic expression other than a few so-called primitive artifacts to give credance to the idea that a civilized human society might have actually existed in the country. Where such cave paintings or carvings were found, they were considered to be crude and uncivilized, the pallid reflections of a primitive mentality unable, or unwilling to embrace the idea of material progress. To the untutored eye of these ethnocentric Europeans, the Australian landscape was utterly 'empty', devoid of beauty, a living hell on earth.

Such a view underwent change only very slowly. Later generations of settlers of course eventually warmed to what they called 'wide open spaces' or the 'land beyond goodbye', accepting this emptiness as an increasingly attractive alternative to the vision of a cluttered industrial landscape filled with 'dark satanic mills' that was beginning to grow up all over Europe. More and more too these early colonial settlers had begun to desert the fragile townships along the coast and head inland, hoping to discover for themselves a paradisal environment that they could call 'home'. The Edenic state loomed large in their minds as they pressed further into the unknown, looking for what was officially termed *New Country*. A frontier mentality quickly developed which regarded the acquisition of land as tantamount to success and happiness. People were not content

to work the country as the Aborigines had done before them —
that is, as hunter-gatherers and nomads; but rather, they were
anxious to portion the land into legally sanctioned allotments
which would remain in their possession in perpetuity. Thus the
Rule of Law had reconstituted the landscape into an intricate
patchwork of surveyed grids that bore no relationship to the
natural contours of the land itself.

Yet still the illusion that the continent represented a pristine
environment remained. The growth of townships, bush roads,
homesteads, mines or pastoral holdings could not really change
the face of this remarkably lonely and isolated land. People
chose to live in it for a time, exploit its natural resources for what
they were worth, but they nearly always decided to retreat from
what Pascal called its 'infinite spaces' at the end of their lives to
the security of established cultural centres like Sydney or
Melbourne or even back to the Mother Country across the
ocean. For the most part the country was considered to be 'not
fit for white man' except as an extension to his materialistic
urge. The dreamers were not those who viewed the land as
sacred, but those who were able to work it for their own
profit.

Such a landscape could not unleash upon the new settlers
what the Aborigines call its *kurunba*, or life-essence. This numen
figured largely in the philosophic and religious beliefs of the
original inhabitants, particularly in relation to the earth itself.
What they saw in their land was not an endless repetition of
'wide open spaces' but a profoundly metaphysical landscape
capable of expressing their deepest spiritual yearnings. What
was prejoratively called 'Blackfellas' country' by Europeans was
to the Aborigines living there the very embodiment of sacred
topography. In other words, the sacred precinct or *temenos* was
not necessarily represented by an architectural structure in
keeping with the Euro-centric perception of a sacred place.
Instead it was reflected in the totality of landscape — that is, the
earth, rock-forms, trees, plains, mountains, insects, animals
etc., and finally in man himself. The bond that linked all these

entities together lay in the mythological and symbolic data that these entities represented as part of the Dreaming Cycle or Primordial Event.

Thus what to the early European settlers of the country was little more than a pristine landscape, was for the Aborigines a complex and luminous spiritual edifice reminiscent of an open-air cathedral. They were not living in a lonely and desolate place, but in an environment conducive to wellbeing and happiness provided that the land be respected for the icon that it was. Of course, such a close identification with landscape and the subsequent formulation of a ritual-based cosmology inevitably lead to accusations of pantheism, totemism and animism being levelled at Aboriginal hierophants. These were belief-systems derived from so-called empirical observations made by anthropologists who were anxious to explain away the existence of any sophisticated spiritual understanding among Aborigines. It was not possible, according to these observers, to believe that there might be other ways of making contact with the numen, or the divine aspect, except via recognized canonical law or even better, via scientific materialism. The stage had been set for the denudation of a spiritual landscape more devastating than if it had been destroyed by an atomic bomb.

It is at this point that we must begin to look at how a landscape transcends its 'pristine' state in order to become an example of what may be termed cultural or sacred topography. The aboriginal belief is that before the Dreaming or *tjukuba* — that is, before the Primordial Event had occurred — this pristine landscape was represented by an unending, featureless plain. In this sense the landscape was pristine since it conformed to the idea of 'chaos' (lit. formless void). Not until the period of *tjukuba* or Dreaming and the mysterious appearance of Sky Heroes, either from inside the earth itself or from an ill-defined upper region, did the landscape take on a truly cosmic significance and attain to Form. At the conclusion of the Dreaming period the Sky Heroes disappeared from the face of the earth, leaving in their place their personalized 'signatures' in the guise of

25

topographic landmarks, contour variations, trees, animals — in fact, all manifestations of life on earth. Such a remarkable event as the Dreaming however must not be confused with the advent of a Golden Age. It was simply a Primordial Event devoid of any qualitative associations that are normally appended to world-creation, or to those who might have been responsible for initiating the event in the first place.

Thus we begin to perceive that the land as we know it has changed. It is no longer the 'land beyond goodbye' so popular among romantic balladists of European origin. In its place we begin to recognize a cultural landscape steeped in *kurunba*, or life-essence. We must take care too not to translate 'life-essence' as a sort of animistic spirit that gives life to the earth in the form of an ingestive/breathing mode such as exists in organic nature. This is to down-grade Aborigines' powers of empirical observation which in practice they possess to an acute degree. *Kurunba* or 'life essence' is a metaphysical expression denoting the presence of a cultural layer within the landform itself that has been inspired by mythological contact with the Dreaming. In other words, the landform has become iconic in essence, fulfilling a role of containment, not only of physical attributes (shape, texture, mineral content etc.), but of *meta*-physical significations. It is this quality that Aborigines term as *kurunba* — that is, the power that gives a landmark its inherant Form over and above that of its mere physical presence.

The Sky Heroes who invested the landscape with *kurunba* through their world-creating activity were true spirit-beings in possession of both divine, human and animal characteristics. When speaking of the hare-wallaby people or the wood-gall people, for example, it is often assumed that these spirit-beings were no more than anthropomorphisms of existing animals. To the European mind, such a way of perception implied a child-like mentality on a par with a peasant folklore obsessed with elfs, gremlins and gnomes. True spirituality, or indeed genuine metaphysical expression, could not be expected with the use of such primitive metaphors since these suggested a 'downward' movement towards dissolution, not an 'upward' movement towards what is eternal. Thus the idea that perhaps such spirit-beings as the hare-wallaby or wood-gall people might embody complex metaphysical truths pertaining to creation, existence and the after-life were dismissed as a deliberate attempt at 'mystification' of what was no more than a basic animistic belief. Aboriginal recognition of their land as a sacred temple, and the spirit-beings who created it as bearers of numen, was regarded also as a deliberate attempt to 'desacralize' the laws governing property possession and the right of ownership as enshrined in European law.

It remains for us now to analyse just how a landscape becomes a cultural topography, and how it relates back to the beings that exist on it and *in* it. For it is not only a cultural topography for man alone; all nature shares in its significations, be they birds, insects, animals, flora or fish. Aboriginal people considered this to be an article of faith: their lives and that of the rest of nature interacted in a way that did not attribute to either a level of primacy. Indeed, Aborigines had no conception of themselves as the 'crown' of God's creation in the way that world religions often deify man. Life *per se* was a web of interactive particles, of which mankind and nature were co-equal partners. Therefore the role of mankind in the drama of life was to re-create through ritual and ceremony the eternal moment of the Dreaming by calling upon the assistance of all nature, whether it be organic or geological. Any dichotomy between man and nature was regarded as an accident, a product of the hiatus between mankind and his knowledge of the Dreaming, not an eternal severance as suggested by the time-lapse that separated mankind from the Primordial Event itself.

Tribal land then became a living entity insofar as it contributed to the overall sustenance of life. What transpired from this unique relationship was that the land *needed* the active cooperation of man in order to fulfil itself as a cosmic principle, in the same way that man needed the land to realize his own cosmogenic self. From such a symbiosis grew up *illud tempus* a need to ratify this relationship through ritual and ceremony so that a bridge could be built between the mundane and supra-mundane worlds. In other words, the earth *as much as mankind* was required to participate in ritual acknowledgement of its sacral existence in order to 'live' and bear fruit. This is why the Aborigines were deeply concerned that the ceremonial cycle each year should be completed correctly and with due reverence; they knew that if this did not happen then the earth would 'harden', and as a result might fail to enact its full fructive possibilities. Drought, flood, disease, scarcity of game etc. occurred not as a natural process but as a failure on the part of man and earth to observe their ritual bonding one with another, and with the Dreaming.

Out of this came a concept of embuing the landscape with numinous landmarks. It meant that from the time of the Dreaming the land as an embodiment of the Sky Heroes' world-creating effort would become an iconic representation of that event. In other words, Aborigines were content to regard their tribal lands as a symbolic landscape. Nor is it safe to say that they invested their country with sacred significance after the Primordial Event. Because the mythological data associated with the landscape in the form of songs and stories was not invented by Aborigines, but was handed down to them from the Sky Heroes themselves by way of their ancestors. The culture of the landscape — that is, the sacred or primordial history attributed to a region — was a reality of other-worldly dimension and a gift that had been passed on to the Aborigines to be treasured in perpetuity. The contrast here between the culture of landscape and European property laws leads us to draw an inevitable conclusion: that the former is a metaphysical gift held in trust by a people dependant upon it for survival; while the latter is a physical acquisition that can be utilized for personal profit or gain.

The interdependance of myth and landscape then became the *modus operandus* for a clear definition of cultural identity. The

Aborigines recognized how important the land was as a mnemonic device to help them recall events from the Dreaming. Since their culture was largely an oral one, it was important for them to have at least an imagistic point of reference from which to reinforce their traditional contact with their ancestors, and with the *tjukuba*. Like the Chinese written character whose philological origins lie in the active event, the verb, rather than in the noun (eg. the character for 'east' embodies the sun rising from behind a tree) it was important for the Aborigines to develop a set of characters, a visual syntax, able to support both cosmogenic and metaphysical belief. At this point landscape became an important co-respondent in the dialogue between man and earth. The language of signs, perceived by man in response to the need to express a cosmogenic or metaphysical reality, was the contribution made by the landscape to this dialogue. A visual language had been created out of rocks, contours, flora, fuana etc. that would enable man to converse with Sky Heroes and so re-create the eternal moment of the Dreaming.

The stage had now been set for the transformation of landscape from its pristine state before the occasion of the Primordial Event into what Leo Frobenius called the creation of a 'paideuma' at the conclusion of the Dreaming. The paideuma being 'the tangle of inrooted ideas'[1] or 'the gristly roots of ideas' that are the bedrock of any culture. According to Mencius epistomology, the men of old (ie. the ancients) wanted to clarify and diffuse the light which comes from looking straight into the heart of things and then acting. By looking 'straight into the heart' of the physical world, the Aborigines were able to discover for themselves a profoundly symbolic language capable of untangling these inrooted ideas so that they could exist in relative harmony with themselves and their environment. At this point landscape had transcended itself as a metaphor only for Creation, for the *tjukuba*, and become instead a part of the Tradition. Landscape had completed its monumental journey from its primordial state of 'chaos' — from its

29

'pristine' condition, that is — to that of active participant in the creation of culture.

From now on the landscape had become a rich source of information on the sacred. Once the ritual keys had been found, the doors to the world of *tjukaba* and its pantheon of spirit-beings and sacred events could be revealed in all their splendour. It was no longer a 'dead' world that Aborigines lived in, a barren continent of 'wide open spaces' driven to alienating man from himself or his environment. It had become instead a manifold mytho-poetic edifice that he could enter into in times of cultural renewal. Such a collusion implied that the land *had a story to tell* to mankind, and all men had to do was listen. In this case what they heard was not only the 'tale of the tribe' but the entire genesial experience. Their own culture and the culture of the Sky Heroes were written into this land in a miraculous way, suggesting a divine intervention, an ordering, that precluded any need for amendment or change. In other words, so complete and so final was the Dreaming event that there was no necessity to look upon the natural world as being in any need of re-arrangement. It was, as far as the Aborigines were concerned, a sacred world and therefore perfect.

We begin to see at this point the seeds of conflict between two opposing cultures existing in the same landscape. On the one hand we have an Aboriginal culture that regards the landscape as an existential partner to which it is lovingly enjoined; on the other, we find a European culture dissatisfied with the landscape's perceived vacuity and spiritual aridity, thus wanting to change it in accordance with facile economic imperatives so that it reflects a materialistic world-view. The gristly root of ideas embodied in the landscape — its paideuma, that is — which had been nurtured by the Aboriginal people since the Dreaming was now under threat of destruction by a race of people that had forsaken its own culture on the anvil of Cartesian, Comptian and Darwinian pedantry. It was this nexus of ideas that was to be foisted upon a so-called pristine landscape in order that it might be changed to suit a race of cultural nomads unwilling, or unable to settle for long in a paideuma of its own.

We might ask, how does this cultural topography manifest itself? How does the landscape embody the distinctive paideuma of the Aboriginal people in a way that transforms it into valid metaphysical expression? To unravel the web of significance surrounding those historical and hagiographic events pertaining to a given landscape requires the adoption of a mentality that asks us to think in images. As Schwaller de Lubicz informs us through his pioneering research into Egyptian hieroglyphs, we must begin to think symbolically. No longer can we allow nature to speak to us through the dialectic veil of western knowledge that we have allowed ourselves to succumb to since the collapse of esotericism in Christianity during the 14-15th centuries. All this has served to do is divorce us from our primordial intellect and the ability to discern the presence of numenous details that continue to surround us at all times. To recognize in a landcape through ritual enactment and imaginal perception the presence of numen is the means by which the Dreaming can be made manifest *illud tempus* — that is, outside time. Such a mode of intellection is uniquely Aboriginal; and it is this people's greatest contribution to their own survival throughout the passage of untold millennia. Indeed, the Aboriginal culture is probably the most ancient and most resilient culture of all to have existed without ever undergoing the kind of distortion and decline that we associate with decadence. The idea of a 'decadent' Aboriginal culture is a product of modern European influence and thought. Until the arrival of Europeans in the 18th century the Aboriginal culture, which had probably existed relatively unchanged for 40,000 years, continued to provide its members with the spiritual succour so necessary to support a society at the height of its intellectual and social vigour.

We need then to study the way Aborigines looked at their tribal lands, and what they saw. To take the first premise, we must re-assess our attitude towards mythology as being a simplistic, if not 'primitive' form of expression and acknowledge it instead as a complex metaphysical language and a purveyor of Truth. Once we begin to realize that a topographic story illicited from a given landscape by a tribal member is not a 'just-so' tale but a demonstration of mythic data, then we will begin to understand what is required of us if we are to attain to a symbolic mode of thought ourselves. Thus in approaching the great monolith in Central Australia known as Uluru (Ayers Rock), we are immediately confronted with a physical entity in the form of the Rock itself, as well as a metaphysical presence in the form of the myths associated with it. Of course, the Rock has been formed by the active agents of weathering, geologic upheavel etc, but only as a result of the intervention by Sky Heroes. According to Aboriginal belief, nature does not function in accordance with arbitary laws but is under the auspices and direct guidance of supernatural beings who themselves are the manifestation of numen. The topographic stories that relate to the creation of Uluru are mytho-poetic expressions of how the Rock was created at the time of the Dreaming. They are not, as some might believe, imaginative constructs bestowed upon the Rock in order to 'explain away' the creation of the Rock in the light of a lack of any scientific knowledge by Aborigines.

So we begin to recognize that in the case of Uluru, as in the case of other open-air cathedrals scattered throughout Australia, that the Rock is a metaphysical reality as well as a geological one. Here before us lies the entire cultural embodiment of the tribe, in this case the Pitjandjara tribe of the Central Desert region, and it is to this artifact that we must address our attention if we are to understand the relationship between man, nature and landscape on the one hand, and spirit, culture and tradition on the other. The Rock is both an epic poem for all, a cautionary tale for some, a source of sacred law and ethics for others, and a repository of esoteric knowledge for those few that aspire to the title of *mekigar* (lit. 'man of magic') or tribal hierophant.

To enter into this world, we must first look at some examples that allow us insight into the world-creating process as initiated by the Sky Heroes at the time of the Dreaming. Most of the southern face of the Rock, for example, was created during the battle between the Liru or poisonous-snake people, and the Kunia, or carpet-snake people. According to belief, the Kunia originally journeyed to a sandhill water-hole where Uluru now stands from their country in the east. Here they camped and, at the close of the Dreaming, found themselves transformed into natural features. As boulders or slabs of rock in the gorges, individual members of the Kunia tribe of Sky Heroes (and First People, or ancestors of the Pitjandjara) can be recognized by their symbolic pubic hairs, the kitchen utensils they carry, or the way they sit on the ground.

A battle, however, took place between these people and the Liru, or carpet-snake people, simply because the Liru were a troublesome group of Sky Heroes. Spears were thrown by the young warriors and to this day various desert oaks and sandhills are metamorphosed bodies of the invading Liru. An escaping Kunia woman, Minma Bulari (ie. a married woman), gave birth to a child, thus creating a cave in which a smaller entrance to another cave symbolises the woman's vulva opening into Bulari's womb. Knee-marks of the women who assisted in the birth are seen on the ground nearby. Meanwhile the Liru continued to attack the Kunia, wreaking considerable havoc. A single-handed combat between the Liru leader, Kulikudjeri, and a young Kunia warrior resulted in severe wounding to both Sky Heroes. The young Kunia warrior crawled away losing a great deal of blood as he did so, resulting in a track which is now a watercourse. When the mother of this man heard that her son had been killed, she attacked Kulikudjeri with her digging stick and cut off his nose. This nose is now a huge slab of rock that has split off from the main mass of Uluru. His eyes and nasal passages remain on the rock face to this day. Under his severed nose are streaked water stains which are the transformed blood of the dying Liru warrior.

According to belief the battle did not end there. Another group of Liru warriors surrounded and attacked those Kunia people living about the Uluru waterhole now on top of the Rock. Although many were killed, the Kunia woman who had lost her son, with her husband among others, managed to escape to a camp on the eastern end of Uluru. The tracks made by the escaping people as they tumbled down the fock-face are now the horizontal marks of the rock strata on the northern side of the Rock. In the end, after great fatalities on both sides, the Liru finally abandoned Uluru and set off for another part of the region to wreak more havoc. Wherever they went they were able to get up to more topographic mischief in the same way as they had done at Uluru.

On the surface this much abbreviated story indicates the level of the cosmogenic drama that had been played out at Uluru at the time of the Dreaming. There are numerous sub-plots to the tale, all of them accounting for nearly every important landmark on the southern face. Numerous other stories account for the rest of the Rock's creation, and each of them has its own ritual song-cycle as well as *churingas* or sacred artifacts to act as mnemonic devices during ceremonies. In this way the Primordial Event is fleshed out by the use of mytho-poetry, thereby giving access to the exoteric significance of the Rock for each tribal member, however young or old he or she may be.

But there are numerous levels to such stories. On one level, of course, their's is the epic adventure, the battle between Sky Heroes for supremacy, the rendition of super-human dilemmas which act as archetypes for men to inform themselves by. There is also the expression of various archetypal passions at a supra-mundane level which enable men to clarify their own response to such passions when they crop up in their own lives. In this sense, the stories are meant to be both edifying and didactic. They are edifying in the sense that they give men role-models by which they can measure the conduct of their own behavior. At the same time they are didactic when they seek to inform men of

34

'how' and 'why' things are done in a certain way. The story of the Kunia woman giving birth, for example, would surely act as a primer in the 'Facts of Life' for any child eager to question the origins of the caves in question. Exoteric story-telling had an important role to play in the continuing process of cultural renewal, particularly since the myth-making process had ceased at the end of the Dreaming. While the Sky Heroes seemed to be 'amoral' in a sense, it should be remembered that their exploits are really no different than those of the Olympian gods or the gods of the Vedas. Aborigines recognized the difference between their own personal behavior as social entities and that of the Sky Heroes who were above censure, since they knew that the Sky Heroes' responsibilities for world-creation entailed a far different order of activity than their own.

So the cultural landscape was now spoken for through the medium of myth. It was no longer a pristine landscape but a bibliography of meaning for a people with an enormous capacity for memory and a keen sense of the need to hand on information in the form that it had been received by them in the first place. Nor was the oral transmission of epic and sacred lore something to be taken lightly. The role of storyteller for each Dreaming site around the Rock was always left in the hands of the man who had been 'possessed by' his respective Dreaming, usually at birth. If a man was a hare-wallaby man or a poison-snake man, then it was his task to remember the stories associated with his Dreaming site and pass them onto fellow members of his tribe, or younger initiates, during times of ritual and ceremonial performance at the site itself. As an informant he was expected to render exactly every detail of his fragment of the Dreaming event so that it might be fitted into the whole. And this whole was the subject of important ceremonials when all the various tribes of a region might come together to hear and recount the sacred stories to one another, either through performance (corroboree) or through song.

It is at this point that we must consider how cultural or sacred topography is translated into art. For it is evident that the landscape does not remain a static entity enlivened only by its mytho-poetic 'signatures'. Aborigines have been at pains to re-create what Gerard Manley Hopkins called an 'inscape' by receiving into themselves the rhythms of the land and expressing these in the form of music, sand-painting, cave frescoes, body-painting and the symbolic diagrams more often than not found on *churingas*. When we look at these various art-forms we begin to perceive the profound richness of this dialogue between man and earth. It would appear that far from man determining the aesthetic required to re-create the earth as an art-object, it is the earth that does so. Hence there are only four principal sacred colours that can be used in cave painting, for example: red, yellow, white and black (red and yellow ochre, pipe-clay and charcoal). Moreover, the abstract designs that are used to designate the presence of animals, human activity, physical attributes etc. all derive from their visual appearance on earth. Thus a concentric circle can mean a man with painted decorations on his body. They can also represent the breasts of women. A triple line of parallel marks can mean the body scars on men. They can also indicate the tracks made by hunters. Concentric crescent shapes can mean a camping place whereas a horse-shoe shaped form can indicate a man sitting on the ground. A concentric square suggests a camp-site as well. At the same time a cresent formed from parallel lines can indicate a camp with a windbreak or men lying on the ground.

While the arbitrary use of such designs might suggest some form of confusion, this is not really so. It simply means that within the context of the story itself the design is always recognized for what it is meant to represent. And if it is not, this is because the story is to a certain extent esoteric and therefore requires explanation by the relevant Dream storyteller.

When we study the *churinga*, however, we are confronted by a different order of expression. For the *churinga* is regarded as being a concentrated form of *kurunba*, or life-essence. Aborigines believe that mere physical contact with this sacred object will cause the *kurunba* to flow into them, thus giving them renewed strength and vitality[2]. In other words, the *churinga* is a concentrated version of the Dreaming site that it represents. At the same time it is is an ideogram explaining by the use of abbreviated signs all the details of the Dreaming event that is being celebrated. At Uluru there are twenty-five known *churingas* relating the events associated with five different myths. All these have different designs on them that can be easily deciphered by the hierophants with knowledge of the particular Dreaming event. *Churingas* are hidden in secret places about the Dreaming site and are only produced when a ceremony is being enacted. They act as mnemonic devices with a view to correct orchestration of the actual rituals. At the conclusion of the ceremony, they are wrapped in bark and replaced in their hiding places. Some of these *churingas* are extremely old and, according to their custodians, were received from the Sky Heroes by their ancestors. Thus, like Christian relics, they embody the special power of the numen that is both beneficial to man in the spiritual sense, as well as being contiguous with the Dreaming site and the Primordial Event itself.

When we observe body-decoration we are again confronted with a range of designs that appear to stem from the earth itself. The designs associated with the different Dreaming events are created on the bodies of the hierophants to reflect the presence of the Sky Heroes during important ceremonies. They are made from eagle down, feathers, powdered ochre, and attached to the body with perspiration and human blood secreted from veins in the arm. Body-painting is designed to transform the hierophant from that of an ordinary mortal into a manfestation of the Sky Hero returned to earth. The hierophant's appearance dressed in the body-painting of the Sky Hero signals that the Dreaming has been re-created at the Dreaming site for the duration of the sacred ceremony itself. While a man is so decorated he is no longer 'himself' in the strict sense, but a pure embodiment of the Sky Hero. The designs that he wears again stem from the signatures of the land. It is the aesthetics of earth that determine the complexity of artistic expression much more than the inhibitions placed upon the craftsman by his limited resources. Because he thinks symbolically, he is able to tap the wellsprings of earth with the aid of *kurunba* so that he might express the extraordinary prescience of the numen itself.

Sand painting is another form of visual expression usually associated with important ceremonies held in the Central Desert region. Blood and water are used to harden the ground designated for the ceremonial tableau. To this red and yellow ochre, together with feathers and down are applied in accordance with the image that is being conveyed. These paintings are used as backdrops to the ceremony or as enlarged *churingas* that, for the duration of the ceremony at least, are imbued with *kurunba*. Such paintings become instruments in the fulfillment of sacred ritual in the same way as the altar and wine cup do in the drama of the Christian liturgy.

But whether it is in art, story-telling or song there is also an esoteric significance that operates in parallel to exoteric expression. The drama of Creation according to the Dreaming as conveyed by these various artistic methods conceals a deeper substratum of metaphysical experience. This knowledge is not open to all members of the tribe, nor is it something that a man has a right to know of simply because he has achieved puberty or because he has successfully engaged in warfare. Esoteric information is only revealed to certain members of a tribe who are considered 'sages' or who have undergone various levels of initiation. Invariably *mekigars* are 'men of high degree' in this area of knowledge, but other men are free to attain to it if they so wish. The concept of Aboriginal sanctity is not popular among Europeans because they assign sainthood to recognized forms of religiosity. Nevertheless, Aborigines themselves regard it as an important part of their culture and often invite potential hierophants to join the 'elect' by practising meditation and withdrawing into solitude for long periods. Esoterism, therefore, thrives in an atmosphere of ritual observance. Some secret-sacred ceremonies, for example, cannot be attended or even observed from a distance by tribal members who have not been initiated into this particular esoteric order. Metaphysical truths are never widely disseminated for fear of them being misused or held up to ridicule. The very nature of esoteric information precludes it from becoming 'general knowledge' since its vitality stems from the fact that it must always remain concealed. In any event the complex symbolism of esoteric thought makes it difficult to comprehend, except when the symbolic language has been learned from a qualified hierophant.

Contrary to Western prejudice, however, esoteric information is not a mere litany of magical formulas designed to promote an increase of game in a region, or the advent of rain. Of course, these requests are occasionally made of the Sky Heroes in times of need, but in a way that suggests complicity rather than a direct entreaty to an external spirit-figure. Once again we are confronting a coeval response between man and nature in the face of a mutual dilemma: the rupture of eternal rhythms and the need to re-establish metaphysical as well as physical order. Esoteric information is an essential ingredient in the re-establishment of that order. For it is only by returning to the 'source' of the anguish — that is, to the Dreaming event that orchestrated those physical conformations such as droughts, pestilents, disease etc. — that a measure of comprehension and acceptance can be derived. Such 'knowledge' can then be passed onto tribal members not privy to esoteric information in a way that restores their faith in the cosmic order. It is at this point that most magical events occur. A *megikar* can myster-iously 'bring on' rain, for example, after the recitation of certain magico-ritual formulas because he has managed to source certain information from nature itself by way of his esoteric training.

So we now begin to gain an insight into the idea of landscape as an embodiment of tradition. What Aborigines teach us is that if tradition and culture are not only to survive but renew themselves as vital forces in the perpetuation of mankind, then we must cease to regard the land as a passive principle devoid of sensibility. There are many sacred centres throughout Australia (as indeed the world), and all of them testify to a profound complicity between man and nature. Each centre is a *temenos*, filling a void in the secular environment. They are there as visible reminders to men of their responsibility to nurture mutuality between themselves and their environment. It is only when these conditions are observed that any genuine hiero-phany can take place. The Aborigines, of course, fully recognized their role in this pageant. By sanctifiying their landscape they were able to experience their own personal hierophany, which was for them the Dreaming. It must be remembered that the Dreaming as such is not a religion. Unlike many world religions it does not have an avataric figure at its centre like Christ, Buddha, Mohammed or Confucius. Nor does it have its origins in history as some other religions do. But what the Dreaming does provide is knowledge of the Primordial Event *illud tempus* and in a way that denotes the possibility of full participation in it by the individual. In this sense the Dreaming provides Aborigines with a metaphysical discipline without the need to assume for itself a spiritual primacy as is the case with most other revelationary religions (eg. Christianity, Islam). The Dreaming is, in Dante's words, not so much a place as a state of being. An Aborigine can enter into the Dreaming while he is enacting a ritual event just as if he were the embodiment of a Sky Hero himself.

Indeed such a unique relationship between man and spirit-figure implies a profound insight into the workings of landscape itself. Because it is only in understanding the earth that made him that the Aborigine is able to embark upon his journey through the intricate and often beautiful cultural landscape of his own sacred tradition that is embodied in it. He sees the land as a metaphysical edifice. He understands its spiritual rhythms. And he accommodates himself to its cyclic transitions. Nor does he ask of it to do more than supply him with life-sustenance and a modicum of wellbeing. At the same time he refuses to exploit it beyond its capacity for renewal. Beyond that he resists the desire to change the land because he knows that in doing so he will tamper with its *kurunba* and with the Dreaming event that made it, *illud tempus*.

This is what landscape as tradition means to the Aborigine. It is a quality of spiritual perception and an ability to live in the shade of the Primordial Event as if it were eternally re-occurring. For the rest of us this event is, parodying Rainer Maria Rilke's words, 'the beginning of Terror we're not yet able to bear.'[3]

Notes

1. Ezra Pound. See *The Cantos*.
2. C.P. Mountford. *Ayres Rock: its People, their Beliefs and their Art.*
3. Rainer Maria Rilke. *The First Elegy*. 'For Beauty's nothing/but beginning of Terror we're still just able to bear.' Trans. J.B.Leishman and Stephen Spender.

CHAPTER 3
The Dream Journey

'If we can voyage to the end of the earth and there find ourselves in the aborigine who most differs from ourselves, we will have made a fruitful pilgrimage.'

Thomas Merton

During the 19th century European settlers coined a phrase which was to describe a particular ritual journey that Aborigines made to celebrate and renew their relationship with their 'country'. It was called 'walkabout' and to this day the term implies both moral condemnation of the Aboriginal work ethic and a desultory incomprehension of Aboriginal religious life. If an Aboriginal stockman chose to go walkabout — that is, make a Dream Journey — his employer would inevitably conclude that the man wished to avoid work. Thus an attitude of suspicion was born which pervades any dialogue between white and black Australians even today. For most white Australians who continue to have contact with these people are firmly convinced that the traditional Aborigine has no spiritual life to speak of, and that he lives surrounded by a veil of animist superstition.

Even ethnologists and anthropologists working in the field late last century tended to reinforce this prejudice. A great deal of research has been done since, of course, highlighting familial and tribal relationships, customs, initiatory techniques, ritual life and artistic expression, much of which has centred around survival modes and how most Aboriginal cultural activity is directed towards assuring physical continuity. Such noted anthropologists as R.M. Berndt and A.P. Elkin, while admitting for example that the sacred Wandjina of the Kimberley region of North-west Australia contain sacred energy or power, nevertheless attribute periodic retouching of these cave paintings with a desire for rain[1]. Yet in contrast, Aboriginal custodians of the Wandjina clearly recognize that these spirit

43

representations have a far wider cosmic role[2]. It is this desire to describe the ritual act, whether it may be expressed in painting, song or dance, in essentially materialist terms that calls into question the so-called objectivity of the anthropologist in his contact with the Australian Aborigine. In fact it was stated by one European observer of the Aboriginal people as far back as 1798 that 'no country has yet been discovered where some trace of religion was not to be found. From every observation and inquiry that I could make among these people, from the first to the last of my aquaintance with them (Aborigines), I can safely pronounce them an exception to this opinion'[3]. Since then the Aborigine has been condemned to living a half life on the fringe of white Australian society, regarded by most as barely human and in no way deserving of respect. In the two hundred years since European settlement their numbers have been so reduced, their self-respect so eroded that it would be difficult to find any left today living the full traditional life as of old. The Dream Journey as a ritual act has instead found its substitute in alcoholism and alienation.

These preliminary observations are essential if we are to understand the true nature of the Dream Journey as a cultural affirmation in the face of the inevitable destruction of Aboriginal society today by Western cultural imperialism. Government agencies are pre-occupied with 'solving' the problems that an indiginous race of people present, precisely because they are unable to deal with the inherent metaphysical nature of the Aboriginal way of life. The Aborigine's insistence on the primordial sanctity of his 'country' is not an act of possession in terms of European property laws (as mining companies and graziers are so afraid of) but an act of being possessed by the land itself[4]. Such an 'inversion' of property values, or the value placed upon land as a harbinger of all that is spiritually important in a man's life, is at the root of the current antagonism between mining interests, graziers and government agencies on the one hand and tribal elders on the other. The basis of the Dream Journey for the Aborigine is a ritual cooperation with nature. If a man fails to do his part in maintaining this relationship, he is liable to distance himself from his origins and so destroy the primordial empathy that has always existed between himself and nature. It is a mistake to assume that the reason why an Aborigine makes a Dream Journey is simply to reinforce nature's ability to renew itself. This belief implies a simplistic world-view which the general sophistication of Aboriginal culture in terms of its under-standing of the role of mythology and symbol does not suggest. In fact the Aborigine is highly conscious that his enactment of a Dream Journey involves a personal renewal that reaches far beyond any so-called increase ritual.

There are two levels to the Dream Journey. One is largely a social activity in which participation is encouraged by all the members of a family group. The other is a more personal activity embarked upon alone in order that the individual might experience a closer understanding of his sacred nature. In both cases, however, there is a certain amount of ritual activity designed to encourage a new awareness of environment and the way personal 'country' can inspire a greater understanding of nature itself. If these two dimensions of the same journey were to be compared, then it might be to regard the former as being exoteric or outward and the latter as an esoteric or inward journey. Yet both journeys overlap in their significance because many of the stories, myth cycles, sacred environments (known as 'hot places') and cave paintings are common to both.

The outward Dream Journey is perennial and follows a seasonal movement. While it is evident that such a journey is linked to the disparity of natural increase within a given environment (fruit ripening in one place, the birth of turtles in another, geese laying their eggs at another time and place), it does not mean that any ritual activity engaged in en route is automatically designed to insure that such increase comes about each season. For the journey is cyclical and involves a return to a place of origin each year. It also involves investing normal day-to-day activity with a significance that reaches beyond the practical application currently being invoked. In other words, while the tribal group may be deeply committed to a hunter-gatherer mode of existence, moving from one place to another as food sources exhaust themselves, they are also made fully aware of the underlying reasons for their activity through the recitation of primordial events by way of dancing, story-telling and song.

In the north, for example, in the Aboriginal reserve known as Arnhemland, there are six seasons, not four or even two as in the southern areas of the continent. But unlike our own seasons which formally begin at particular times of the year, the seasonal cycle of the Arnhemlanders is a moveable feast integrally associated with natural events. If these events do not happen for any reason, or are delayed, then the people might perform rituals to enhance their empathy with the natural event — that is, with the failure in the cosmic cycle already observed. To say that they wish *to bring on* the event that has not occurred through ritual activity is to attribute to the Aborigines a niave mechanistic belief in the way nature operates. Yet in terms of empirical knowledge these people are acute observers of natural phenomena and are well aware of how the seasonal cycle manifests itself. They are aware too of how it can break down, and consequently how this ruction can best be expressed at a symbolic level through the use of myth and ritual.

Thus we are not dealing with an unending journey back and forth across tribal territory solely in pursuit of food. Instead we are looking at a sacred journey in which each stage is imbued with sacred significance. The role that ritual and the myth-life of the tribe take in all this as they roam across their Dream landscape is to enhance the significance of what would otherwise be fairly mundane events. One writer has stated that the Aborigine 'moves, not in a landscape, but in a humanised realm saturated with significations'[5]. It is these significations that make the Dream Journey such an important cosmic event in the lives of Aborigines. Each time they make the journey they are encountering what Satose Wanabe explained as 'their entire past existing integrally in their present'.

A tribal elder living near the Arnhemland Escarpment outlined the way the seasonal cycle was differentiated in a recent field trip that we made to the region. Toby Gangele, a member of the Mirarr Kunjai:mi tribe, occupies country that embraces both tropical bushland and vaste swamps that in season are home to countless numbers of magpie geese. In his own words, he explains:

'We have six seasons. But our season don't come regular like they do for balanda (white man). *Yegge* (April-mid June approx) be cool time for us. We know when it begin because *Yamidji* the green grasshopper, he call out that cheeky yams are ready. When *Andjalem* (woolly butt trees) comin' up all over flowers, we know *Wurrgeng* (late June-mid August) cold season starts. T'at time we light fires to burn off undergrowth, make land new again. Come *Gurrung* season (mid August-early October) and all best fruit trees like green plum and white apple comin' up pretty wi' flowers. It hot and dry t'en. Starts to get humid pretty soon as *Gunumelong* (October-December) comin' along. Meantime, rain start fallin' and land all over flooded. We callin' t'is time *Gudjewa* (December-end of March). Magpie geese layin' plenty eggs t'en, and goanna (a lizard) he start callin' from trees. Tribes joinin' us here at about t'is time from far away as Stone Country (Arnhemland) to eat eggs wit' us. It good time t'en. Plenty dancin', singin' songs. When knock-'em-down storms comin' at end of monsoon time, all of us head up into Stone Country durin' *Bang Gerang* (April). After t'at we hear *Yamidji* green grasshopper, he callin' out about cheeky yams once more and we comin' down to wetlands again.'[6]

So the seasonal cycle is completed in terms of the natural cycle. During this time, of course, Toby Gangele and his family would have travelled over a region of approximately 1000 square miles looking for sustenance in a time-honoured way. The route that they had taken would vary little, if at all, from that covered by their ancestors for perhaps thousands of years. At the same time they would have observed a series of rituals entirely governed by the location that they happened to be in. These rituals would vary from place to place, however, depending on the hot places (both positive and negative) that they might have had to encounter along the way. But to use the word 'ritual' does not mean that whatever celebrations, song cycles or stories were invoked along the Dream route had to necessarily conform to some rigid, hieratic formula of expression. Indeed much of the ritual associated with Aboriginal tribal life is spontaneous, even joyous, a product of a people profoundly content within their environment. Only certain ceremonies such as those associated with initiation take on the more formal aspects of what we might consider as a carefully orchestrated ritual act.

The seasonal cycle is a *practical* reason for making a Dream Journey. Toby Gangele and his relatives are well aware of why they make the journey, considering it an important part of their food-gathering activities and a way of coming in contact with other tribal groupings and various relatives. But they are also well aware of another reason for making the journey; a reason integrally associated with their spiritual life. For the land they cross is a part of themselves[7]. The Dream Journey on the ritual level is a way of renewing contact with themselves, since they and the land are inseparable. It is at this point that the Aborigine enters into a Dream world where the land is transformed into a metaphysical landscape saturated with significations. In the same way that Homeric heroes live in close proximity and contact with the Olympian gods, so too do Aborigines recognize the immanent presence of their own spiritual exemplars.

The metaphysical landscape, then, is transformed into an ideal landscape, a hagiographic history of the people's origins, their struggle to survive, how and from whom they received their cultural gifts such as the ability to dance, sing songs, make spears, and hunt during that timeless moment known as the Dreaming. It is timeless because these primordial events took place both in the far distant past before even their ancesters had appeared on the earth — and are continuing to occur even as they are making their Dream Journey in the present[8]. Their encounter with their 'country' as they roam across it is an encounter with spiritual genesis, both personal and collective.

It is at this point that the landscape becomes fully humanised. In other words the Aborigines begin to recognize what the anthropologists refer to as a 'totemic landscape'. Unfortunately the term 'totem' has denegratory connotations associated with an infantile sprirituality, or fetishism, made popular by a whole generation of anthropologists eager to downgrade Aboriginal spirituality in the past. But if we regard a totem in the way that Stanner was at pains to describe it as 'a sufficient condition, not a determinant, or any other relationship. It is a sign of unity between things or person *unified by something else.*[9] Then we begin to perceive the complex symbolism inherent in a Dream landscape. What had previously been linked to a range of food-yielding determinants has now been raised onto another plane altogether.

Along the Arnhemland Escarpment there are vast rock galleries which house some of the finest rock art in the world. Some of the tableaux reflect religious themes, while others are more concerned with secular events such as hunting, animal portraits and general social activity among the clans. Many of these paintings are quite old, their origin reaching back into distant antiquity. Conversely, they are also quite new as they are being continually retouched by tribal elders and custodians of the land in which they appear[10]. All this means that the actual topography has been fully integrated into the speculative belief of the clan members past and present, at least at the symbolic level, as well as acting as a point of identification (ie, a recognizable hot place) in terms of Aboriginal cosmology. The tribal land, the hot places scattered about it, the painting depicting Dreaming events, the mythology derived from individual landmarks such as boulders, trees, waterholes et al — all these contribute to defining the spiritual landscape encompassed in the Dream Journey itself.

Throughout the journey the clan members come into contact with evidence of their spiritual ancestry. At Deaf Adder Creek (Arnhemland), for example, they must cross the watercourse in order to make their way to Goose Camp where they will hunt magpie geese and collect eggs. But they do not simply swim the creek. Instead they enlist the aid of the Rainbow Serpent, a world-creating entity that figures very largely in the mythology of Aborigines throughout Australia. Quite often a waterhole may be the precise spot where the Rainbow Serpent or similar Sky Heroes re-entered the earth after their world-creating effort at the time of the Dreaming. Cullymurra waterhole on the Cooper Creek in Central Australia is one such place. To the Dieri tribesmen it was known as the 'Hole of Life' and represented a powerful hot place filled with all the import of world-creation itself[11].

The Dream Journey is in a sense a replication of the world-creating trek of the Rainbow Serpent and other Sky Heroes because all the topographic landmarks feature in this primordial event that occurred at the time of Dreaming. At Djuwarr lagoon, for instance, on the Escarpment, the Rainbow Serpent is reputed to have split the cliff-face on its way up the gorge to a deep pool below a waterfall. Here the Snake disappeared. Though no longer manifest, the Rainbow Serpent's presence has embued not only the gorge which it has created with sacred significance, but also the pool where it disappeared. Until recently, each year at this spot both the Mirarr and Badmardi tribes gathered to perform important ceremonies in honour of the Great Snake's world-creating efforts. In so doing they were able to renew contact with the Dreaming, re-inforcing at the same time their own participation in such an important metaphysical event.

Other spots, however, have been created by lesser spirit

entities such as the Mimi people — a small, wraith-like people shaped in the image of thin sticks who have the power to re-emerge from the rock-face on which they are so often painted. Aborigines are in awe of these spirit-people since they can alternate between a state of benevolence or that of deliberate malignity whenever they choose. It is this ambivalence that make them genuine spirits rather than allegorizations of natural forces such as the anthropologists might have us believe. At the same time the Mimi only appear when there is silence and can be invoked only if one is susceptible to their presence. If one breathes too hard, or a wind suddenly blows up, the Mimi are liable to be broken into little bits[12]. It is this state of spiritual readiness that characterizes the Dream journeyer whenever he wishes to invoke the Mimi and so enter more fully into a relationship between himself and these spirit people[13].

Of course, animals and fauna in general play an important part in world-creation as well. In the Central Desert region inhabited by the Arunta people, one observer discovered a series of sacred sites linked to the Dream Journey of the red kangaroo (the First Beast of its species). This in turn had inspired a number of ceremonies and songs depicting the supernatural trek of the original red kangaroo, Kolakola, as it moved across the landscape[14]. In a highly evocative song cycle the journey is detailed, culminating in the celebration of a particular hot place where the red kangaroo was reputed to have disappeared.

> 'I Kolakola, am hurrying on without delay;
> From my hollow I am hurrying on without delay.
> I, the young kangeroo, am journeying
>   a far journey without a halt;
> Leaving behind a thin trail I am journeying
> on a far journey without a halt.'

The song cycle concludes:

> 'Hail to thee, Krantji, mother of men!

Be fruitful in the ancestral embrace,
Filled with game for the use of men!
The crutch fat is gleaming white,
The crutch fat is white like sand
The Rock-plate quivers as the avengers arrive:
Our Rock-plate of white fat —
Our Rock-plate is quivering, our Rock-plate
    is quivering and stirring.
Our wind-break home of white fat —
Our wind-break home that gleams like sand'.

Such songs as this one depict primordial events which have occurred right across inland Australia in the guise of localized mythologies. They celebrate the relationship between men and nature in a way that dignifies the celebrant, while at the same time they help to create a cogent mythological landscape important to the preservation of Aboriginal culture in general. Yet in contrast, one contemporary ecologist has been at pains to describe this journey in terms of what he calls 'eco-mythology'[15]. In a contradictory paragraph he notes: 'The relationship between methods of passage and the habitat preferences of kangaroos pursuade me also that it is no accident (ie. the Dream Journey taken by the red kangaroo, Kolakola). The best habitat was traversed by *natural means* (our italics) and created thereby, and the worst habitat, *supernaturally.* . . . The ancient Aborigines who created these legends must have been well-acquainted with the ecology of the red kangaroo, and appear to have passed that knowledge into mythology to be hidden by allegory'. In spite of 'passing knowledge into mythology to be hidden by allegory' whatever that is meant to mean, it is difficult to understand why the Aborigines would wish to distinguish between natural and supernatural means of travel when describing a Dream Journey when, according to the author, they were already familiar with the ecology of the red kangaroo. Indeed it is this kind of confusion that has plagued any fuller understanding of

Aboriginal spirituality and has ultimately lead to the dismissal of the Dream Journey, along with its incorporated hot places or sacred sites that litter the country, as a metaphysical event of any significance at all. Instead we are dealing here with reductive analysis designed to destroy permanently a super-natural event in the interests of modern science and the secular state bent on annexing sacred sites, and indeed all Aboriginal tribal lands, for future mining development.

The outward journey explores a number of certitudes at different levels. There is the constant search for nourishment, of course, which is a practical concern for all the clan members. This concern is often identified with particular landmarks where traditionally food has always been found. However, such landmarks also exist within a symbolic landscape and invoke ceremonial activity as the clan is passing through a particular region. If a clan leaves its own country in order to link up with neighbouring clans on the occasion of important ceremonial activity, there are songs that poignantly render the sense of loss experienced at this separation.

> 'Hands swinging, swinging, Wurei
> walks quietly away from Miningdjabu.
> Maiawulu and Maiamaia both look ahead
> as they leave Burarineibu.
> They follow the bushes, the stones and trees
> looking for signs in the sharp grass.
> Over flat stones, past high cliffs
> they walk to open ground.'

Then the spirit people recall where they have come from:

> 'Looking back at the cliffs, towards
> the long hills, and Bunggarindji,
> towards Wurei and Laglag as we move
> along the gully to the plains,
> I am overcome with sadness
> as we leave camp — those stone hills
> at Darngaua and that cliff-face known as Blaweru.

> As we follow the red kangaroo's path
> across the open plain,
> the loss of my own place makes me sad
> as I stood on the open plain
> hoping for rain.'

In such a song there is both a feeling of sadness as a result of the exodus from their personal country, as well as a feeling of profound love for the very stones that make up this country. One also senses a relationship between these spirit people making the journey (in which men inevitably identify) and the land itself — as if they are essentially made up of the same substance.

The outward journey culminates in a cyclical return. From this point the tribal member has entered into what Stanner called the symbolic complex 'one flesh-one spirit-one country-one Dreaming'[16]. He has sought and experienced spiritual renewal through participation in the Dream Journey. He has witnessed once again a symbolic landscape that is both personal in terms of his own growth, and collective in terms of identification with his ancestors. He has participated in the world-creating process as it was enacted during the Dreaming, or Great Time. And in the process, he has engaged in a ritual act of identification with his country similar to Goethe's observation: 'Man knows himself insofar as he knows the world, becoming aware of it only within himself, and of himself only within it'. This is only the beginning of the outward journey, yet in it are the seeds of the inward journey which will be explored in detail in the following chapter.

Notes

1. R.M & C.H. Berndt, *The World of the First Australians*. 'The Wandjina are mythical beings, male and female, the great creators and guardians responsible for the continuing welfare of the local Aborigines; and around them are drawn the totemic beings and creatures, on which these people depend for sustenance . . . the ritual act of painting or touching them releases sacred energy or power, bringing on the wet season . . .'

A view from one of the caves in Obiri Rock, Arnhemland Escarpment area. Many of these caves have been overpainted by successive generations since the first inhabitants arrived over the land bridge from Asia, 50,000 years ago. Obiri Rock, like Nourlangie and Uluru (Ayers Rock), is an 'Open-air Cathedral' recording the sacred images of the Aboriginal culture.

Lightning Man, Nourlangie Rock. Note the tiny axeheads protruding from his body and limbs. These, clashing against the heavens, create lightning during the rainy season, a pontifical statement nevertheless from the Dreaming.

Lightning Man, Namargin, painted in the X-ray style unique to this region of Australia. His 'inner' body is revealed in its physiological exactitude as well as a patterned work of art.

Barramundie fish and Spirit Figures, Nourlangie Rock. Without facial expression, these Spirit Figures are iconic representations of spirit types rather than individual people.

Male tribesman painted in the 'stick' style, an earlier style to that of X-ray. He is carrying hunting equipment such as spears and a stone axe, as well as dilly bags.

Part of the main frieze, Nourlangie Rock, depicting a confrontation between Lightning Man and his wife (*top figure*) and Namanjolk, a malign Spirit Figure. This frieze was retouched by Barramundie Charlie some 20 years ago. Since then he has died. It is unlikely that any of his friends have the technical expertise to renew this remarkable painting. Unfortunately, ritual renewal by surviving members of the tribe has so far failed to re-occur. If this situation should continue, then the *djang* of this important hot place will eventually diminish.

Barramundie fish and female Spirit Figure painted in the X-ray style, Nourlangie Rock.

Sea turtle painted in the X-ray style. Turtles are speared in the ocean off the coast of Arnhemland.

2. Crawford, *The Art of the Wandjina*. 'Wandjina djini jeijo: ru. Dambun djuman mumana'. (transl. Wandjina is the important one. He made the world.) Attributed to Mowaldjali, a Narinjin tribesman of the Kimberley region.

3. David Collins, *An Account of the English Colony in New South Wales*.

4. Tribal elder's remarks: 'We do not say that the land belongs to us, but that we belong to the land'.

5. W.E.H. Stanner, *White Man got no Dreaming*, Essays 1938-1973.

6. Author's field notes, 1983.

7. 'The people of the whole country are one. George used to go all over the area to fetch Butcher Knight and take him to his place for awhile. They are all one company, one mob.' George Namingum, tribal elder.

8. What Mirca Eliade calls *illud tempus*, or the Great Time. *Myths, Dreams and Mysteries*.

9. Ibid.

10. Crawford, *The Art of the Wandjina*. 'Because you are looking so dull — you're not looking bright — I'll try and draw you. I'll try and put new paint on you people to make you new again. Don't get wild, *don't send rain!* (cf. Bernt's remarks in NOTE 1). You must be very glad that I am going to make you new again'. Attributed to tribal elder, Charlie Numbulmoore.

11. This waterhole is the largest and deepest in Australia. In 1861 the explorers Burke and Wills (who had crossed the continent from north to south) both died here in the midst of an abundance of wildlife.

12. According to Toby Gangele.

13. Cf. Henry Thoreau, 'We must learn to reawaken ourselves and keep ourselves awake, not by mechanical aids, but by an infinite expectation of the dawn, which does not forsake us in our soundest sleep'.

14. T.G. Strehlow, *Aranda traditions* 1947.

15. A.E. Newsome, *The Eco-mythology of the Red Kangaroo in Central Australia*, Mankind, December 1980, Vol.12 No 4.

16. Ibid.

CHAPTER 4
Pilgrimage of the Soul

In the previous chapter emphasis was placed upon the more exoteric aspects of the Dream Journey as a way of fulfilling sacred obligations in terms of the landscape — that is, personal or tribal country — as well as that of the traditional encounter with age-old food sources.. It was established also that aside from food requirements the Dream Journey embarked upon each year by Aborigines was a replication of world-creating events that took place at the time of Dreaming. Thus the topographic landmarks, or hot places, that they observed along the way were noetic points contingent to a metaphysical landscape that had been divinely constructed by Sky Heroes such as Lightning Man and the Rainbow Serpent, the Mimi people and the First Animals among others. The creation of tribal land through the activity of the Sky Heroes making their sacred Dream journeys, then, was not only a microcosmic event relative to the individual or clan concerned, but also macrocosmic insofar as such an event had occurred both inside and outside time. In other words, these world-creating events still occur whenever there is Aboriginal participation in them via ceremony and ritual.

Which leads us to the inward or esoteric Dream Journey that is principally the exclusive preserve of the menfolk within the tribal community. It is a ritual act intimately associated with making contact with a man's Dreaming, with his primordial ancestors, and with his totem or spiritual alter ego. For it is only when he makes this journey, often alone or at least with fellow initiates, that he begins to perceive his relationship with the unmanifest powers embodied in his mythological heroes. An analogy to the inward Dream Journey might be found in an early Christian pilgrimage route (the Via Dolorosa), or in the more ritual sense — recitation of the Stations of the Cross or the Jesus Prayer in Eastern Orthodoxy. Though it must be emphasised that this is only an analogy and implies no similarity among the respective spiritual disciplines even if they are found to exist.

One myth related among north Australian tribes tells in striking detail of an important Dreaming event. A great man, Angamunggi, was treacherously killed by his son who had already committed incest with his sisters. The son, Tjinimin, was filled with guile, malice and lust. Having seduced his sisters, he next speared his father while he was sitting surrounded by his children enjoying a festive moment during a gathering of all the clans. In agony and about to die, the father nevertheless lingered on to perform a series of marvels. *He moved from place to place and in doing so formed a track or path which is now sacred* (our italics). At each resting place he tried without success to staunch the flow of blood from the spear wound in his side. In some mysterious way his blood produced perennial pools and springs of water, which remain today as his marks or signs upon the land. After a long trek he took all the fire then present in the world, tied it on his head with his own hair, and waded into the sea. At the last moment another man courageously snatched a brand from his head just as Angamunggi was about to disappear beneath the waves. In this way fire was saved for men who would have otherwise have been forced to eat raw food, like animals. Even in his death agonies, however, Angamunggi had given men perennial, life-giving waters in which he also placed the spirits of all those children who have been born since then[1].

Even at its primary symbolic level this myth finds echoes in Christological and Osirian cosmology. One cannot help noticing iconic parallels with the Crucifixion and the subsequent bestowal of the 'waters of eternal life' by way of the shedding of blood. Even if these parallel religious motifs are intuitional, they are no less real for being so. But what is important in this myth is the italicized remark suggesting the primacy of the sacred journey at the very moment when mankind was receiving what Stanner called the 'metaphysical gift' — that is, the ability to transcend oneself[2]. For it is this gift that becomes the object of the inward Dream Journey for all Aboriginal initiates. Among other things they are journeying in order to experience an epiphany.

This journey, however, is both lineal and metaphysical. While it is important for initiates to visit Dreaming sites (hot places) in order to perform ceremonies, there are times when the Dreaming site can be invoked simply by declaring an area sacred for the duration of these ceremonies. This is done by mounting a watchman on a high rock to warn off approaching intruders. Once a site has been declared sacred, then the initiates are able to perform their 'big rituals' much as they might have done if they had been located in the region of the actual Dreaming site itself. Such spontaneous ceremonial activity usually occurs when the men are outside their territory, or when the territory has long since been encroached upon by white graziers, making a return to it difficult for one reason or another.

Though a great deal of importance is attached to the actual hot place itself, particularly because of the power or *djang* that it might possess, this power is implicitly expressed in the ceremonies themselves when a group of initiates happen to be performing at a fabricated sacred Dreaming site. In other words, the ceremonial function will be no less effective because it happens to be performed not at the actual hot place itself. The important point in all this is the principle, not the accident of location. Initiates clearly identify the inner landscape as being more important than the country over which they might be traversing, even if this also has a sacred significance in terms of what it represents. The initiate, whether he be alone or in a group, knows that he can recreate the conditions conducive to entering the Dreaming — that is, experiencing for himself the epiphanic state that is one of the objects of the Dream Journey.

A.P. Elkin[3] outlined a 'big ritual' he observed in north-western South Australia sometime in 1930 in response to his inquiry about the Dreaming. After a sacred precinct had been made, the men sat on the ground in two ceremonial rings. They then proceeded to sing a series of chants to the rhythm of sticks vigorously beaten on the ground. In the meantime two performers disappeared for an hour or so behind a clump of bushes in order to paint and decorate themselves. While they did so the singers continued to invoke the names and achievements of Sky Heroes and their ancesters to the point where the presence of these spiritual entities was strongly felt by all those participating in the ceremony. At a critical moment when the chanting had reached its climax, Elkin was asked not to look up suddenly in case he might destroy the epiphanic event being played out before him. Only when the performers had appeared from behind the bush and commenced their enactment of the mythical event was he told that the men were in a state of Dreaming — that they had 'become' the Sky Heroes and First Animals already described in the chants and songs. Not only had the men dancing transcended themselves, but also those who had invoked the Dreaming by recitation of these primordial events through their music and song.

Contact with the Dreaming is the sole object for all the participants during these ceremonies. It is not a divine *place* that they are endeavouring to enter by way of ritual gesture, but a state of mind — a return to the source. All acts embodied in the Dream Journey, whether they involve visiting hot places or sanctifying space at any given locality, are designed to create conditions acceptable to the emergence of Sky Heroes from the Dreaming. It is therefore important that the initiates concerned acknowledge the presence of these spirit entities through the use of complex symbolism and ritual activity designed to bring on an ecstatic or epiphanic state. Only then can it be said that the initiates have transcended the relativity of the exoteric or outward Dream Journey in their quest for a greater degree of spiritual empathy with the realm of Dreaming.

C.P. Mountford[4] once described a Dream Journey dedicated to Jarapiri, the Great Snake, that he experienced in the company of an Aboriginal of the Walbiri tribe in Central Australia. It is a remarkable document outlining the exact route that Aboriginal initiates must take when celebrating the world-creating activity of the Great Snake at the time of Dreaming. While there is a physical journey involved, encompassing a trek of more than 100 miles in length, there is also a ceremonial route that must be taken as well. Such a route involves a complex set of rituals, body-paintings and the recitation of various song-cycles at different hot places along the route. These songs recall not only the activity of Jarapiri as he moved along, but also that of other spirit-figures that feature in the mythology of the Dream Journey itself.

A typical Jarapiri song details the creation of certain landmarks in the form of the movement of a snake:

> 'Jarapiri's ribs move him along,
> he leaves a meandering track.
> Jarapiri's ribs move him along,
> he leaves a meandering track etc.'

In contrast, there are other songs dedicated to mythical insects or animals integral to the world-creating process such as Mamu-boijunda, the Great Spider:

> 'Mamu-boijunda, great spider barking
>   in dawn light.
> Risen creatures come strange, light-filled
>   into this world.
> Mamu-boijunda, great spider crying —
> Latalpa snakes and death-adder women
>   inhabit the dawn.
> Mamu-boijunda, his task completed,
> rests among his creations on Winbaraku —
>   snakes and insects all.'5

There is also an invocation which suggests that the initiate is extremely conscious of the process, and sacred import, of creation as originated by the Great Snake, particularly when it comes to a declaration of that activity with the aid of ritual gesture and invocation. The words, 'Balga-ma-ni!' (Bring all into being) indicate the extent to which the initiate acknowledges the world-creating role of the Great Snake and other spirit entities even as he participates in the process himself. This is confirmed in the following song:

'Great Snake, Jarapiri, singular being
wander Walbiri earth.
Great Snake, Jarapiri, give name
to all Walbiri plants.
Great Snake, Jarapiri, wind source
with rain on your forked tongue.'[6]

In this way the landscape is humanized through a series of song-cycles dedicated to Jarapiri and the spirit people who accompanied him across Walbiri country. The initiate's role in all this is to recreate the journey that the Sky Heroes once made. As well as walking in the path of Jarapiri, he is also required to engage in ritual body painting suitable to the different sites visited, and to the different spirit entities invoked. Thus he will body paint himself in the symbols of the great Snake, or perhaps Mamu-boijunda, the Great Spider, depending on which hot place he is visiting. This form of activity helps to enhance the separation of the initiate from the mundane world in order that he might experience an epiphany. Of course, this does not always happen. Like all rituals they tend to become an end in themselves when merely mouthed as ancient formulas. Yet the possibility for epiphany is always latent and really only depends upon the level of commitment of the initiate concerned. For the man who undergoes initiation as an adolescent and later as a full warrior under the auspices of fellow tribesmen and elders, there is also the possibility of undergoing a third stage of initiation that is both voluntary and, to a certain extent, entirely contemplative. A man will rarely embark upon such a Dream Journey until he has fulfilled most of his social duties within the tribal context.

Nor does he do it alone — at least, he is responsible to a qualified person or guide when he embarks upon such a journey, possibly alone. Such an 'Order' of men of knowledge depends on an unbroken succession of qualified persons. These men are known as 'clever men', or men of 'high degree'[7].

Unfortunately, what little material there is on the making of a man of high degree suggest that the process was entirely associated with the creation of a medicine man. Elkin did go so far as to acknowledge that few men of high degree ever spoke English and that as an anthropologist he did not have command of the 'native' language anyway. 'Hence, they (the men of high degree) could not discuss adequately the philosophical and psychological aspects of the triune system of specialist knowledge, faith and ritual, which was the basis of their craft'[8]. It might be suggested here that they could discuss their triune system quite adequately with someone who was both a man of high degree or a postulant, or indeed a man who spoke 'their' language. Because the question of language is at the very heart of the making of a man of high degree.

Indeed the concept of the witch doctor or medicine man is linked almost entirely to the idea of psychic hegemony over the group or individual by way of his ability to deceive, or at the very most his ability to heal various physical and spiritual disorders. Hence the man of high degree is perceived as having a functional role within his community in keeping with the anthropological bias towards seeing Aboriginal society in terms of its empirical requirements. Such an approach has lead to the man of high degree being partly dismissed as a genuine hierophant whose principal responsibility is not only to act as a model within the context of his tribe and heal the sick when his services might be required, but also to preserve the sacred mysteries which, after all, are the tribe's metaphysical patrimony entrusted to him for safe-keeping. So that the terms 'clever man', 'witch doctor' and 'medicine man', though probably rough translatory meanings made by Aborigines initially to describe the principle and function of the man of high degree within their society, have since become reductive in tenor. A man of high degree is subsequently regarded as being at the very least a trickster, a manipulator and a practitioner of magical arts rather than a genuine hierophant, or possibly even — a saint.

This is important to appreciate as the idea of the sanctified man within the context of a traditional society like that of Aborigines is virtually unheard of. Some concessions have been made to Aboriginal spirituality in the guise of animism or panthiesm, but these have only lead to an assumption of a certain level of primitive belief which is inevitably reductive as well. Yet the reality is that this third level of initiation and the contemplative Dream Journey embarked upon in order to achieve the status of a man of high degree, reaches far beyond the context of merely attaining to the level of a medicine man or clever man. Though a medicine man is invariably a man of high degree, he is also a man who has reached a level of profound spiritual insight in accordance with the ritual belief of his culture. Such men, according to Elkin, possess the knowledge, psychic insight, mystical experience and personal authority that make them worthy members of this sacred Order known as men of high degree. Quite obviously such men, when they have attained to this status, must be similar to what we might know as prophets or saints.

Thus the contemplative or inward Dream Journey no longer places so much emphasis on the physical landscape as in the outward Dream Journey. Hot places remain important, of course, but only as aids to contemplation through ritual activity. This activity is often enhanced by the use of *churingas* as iconic representations of the actual journey taken by the Sky Heroes. A *churinga* is usually made of wood or flattened stone upon which the sacred tracks of the Sky Heroes are carved. These in turn are produced from secret hiding places during ceremonies at the hot place or Dreaming site. When the ceremony has been completed, the *churingas* are returned to their hiding place until the next visitation. What few *churingas* are left are sometimes very old, having been made by the ancestors themselves. They are often kept and used during the ceremonies even when they are breaking up. For they contain *kurunba* or *djang* — that particular spiritual power or emanation associated with life essence. The Aborigines often refer to its emanation as being 'like a mist', so subtle is its appearance. Nevertheless, a *churinga* is much more than a totemic representation as is so often suggested. These sacred objects are primordially created by the Sky Heroes as aids to contemplation for those who wish to use them. As such they partake of the divine essence in the same way as an Orthodox icon might do.

It is clear that this third initiatory stage characterized by the inward Dream Journey has much to do with learning secret rites from older tribal members, and learning how to communicate in a language understood only by spirit entities and fellow initiates. Stanner described this state as a transition into Aboriginal High Culture or entry into the Order. A man of High Degree often no longer speaks in the words of mundane language, expressing himself instead in the mystical language of his ancestors. While we might be tempted to correlate this sacred language with shamanic trance-states among other traditional cultures, this could lead to misinterpretation. The language they speak is the 'language of the Gods' and is only partly related to visionary experience in the ordinary sense. We are looking here at a symbolic language heavily impregnated with the syntax of myth. Only those who fully understand and appreciate the esoteric significance of the myth journey (ie. the Dream Journey) are able to communicate in this sacred language.

In the North-west of Australia in an area known as the Kimberley there is an important but sparely documented doctrine associated with spirit entities known as the Rai. These Rai are said to be spirits-of-the-dead with both male and female characteristics. According to Coate[9] one of their principal tasks is to 'teach' those who wish to become magicians or diagnosticians. The suggestion, of course, is that the Rai have a functional role in keeping with the empirical objectives of the tribe. Yet they are also manifestations of the Wandjina[10] and as such partake of the source in the same way that angels do in Christic and Islamic cosmology. They usually manifest themselves to the ordinary observer in dreams,[11] otherwise they remain invisible except to men of high degree. More importantly perhaps, the Rai are acknowledged as being indispensible to men's wellbeing. They are in a sense guardian spirits. As one Aboriginal informant explained, "The Rai never let us become separated from them. We ourselves don't have pleasure (without them). We might not be a people in this world unless they had stuck to us right through."

It is this spiritual allegiance between the initiate and the spirit entities such as Rai or Mimi people that characterizes an essential aspect of the inward Dream Journey. While it may be true that clever men are on intimate terms with the Rai, it would be a mistake to assume that this relationship is exclusive to the magician. Because the Rai has the power to 'teach' men in the way that an elder or fellow initiate cannot. As our informant says, "The other man says (in his mind) the Rai will help me. The Rai is teaching the man who wants to be a magician." Here we see acknowledged a specific integration between the Rai or spirit entities and the initiate's inner world. He knows that the Rai are talking to him in a language intelligible only to himself at the given point on his Dream Journey. In contrast, ordinary observers are regarded as being ignorant of the Rai. They do not see them because they lack the knowledge to do so. "We are ignorant, we don't see these Rai. They (the Rai) only talk to experts, and only experts know them," says our informant.

So that when an initiate experiences an epiphany, whether it be during the course of an inward Dream Journey or during the process of being made into a man of high degree, he attains to a level of spiritual perception where he is able to 'see' with an inner eye. This eye has been termed a third eye, presumably to identify it with the third eye and its significance in the Eastern religious tradition. In one part of Coate's document we are confronted by a quite explicit and often moving description of the spiritual state of the initiate who has seen the Rai with his inner eye.

'The bodies of the magicians overflow with magic stones called *gedji*. They (the hierophants) can see those different lands. They can see the country underneath. There in the underworld they can see them, bunched up together, they can see them. In the *ungur* place are the only ones we know. The helpless ones — the aged — tell us those stories. Grandfather was telling us and our fathers and (tribal) brothers. These were famous ones, but they have already gone. "There are none today," they said. "They had it that way in the old days when he, this man, was a magician. These things pertaining to the body we call magic stones. They are eating (possessing) the magician. They are eating his blood. They are changing him. We call him an expert because the stones changed him. His flesh becomes light in colour.[12] This one is called an expert. That's how he was separated from the others. It exalted him! Made him a man of high degree. Our bodies are not the same as his. We are ignoramuses. He is different. He becomes light." '[13]

It is evident from this report of the qualitive and physical differences perceived between an ordinary man and a man of high degree that we have at last encountered the epiphanic objective of the sacred Dream Journey. Through the skein of language it is nevertheless possible to recognize a genuine transfigurative experience lying at the core of the actual journey itself, whether this journey is made in the exoteric sense or whether it is the fulfillment of an interior journey made in the course of becoming a man of high degree. To say that Aborigines prior to the collapse of their culture after their contact with Europeans during the past 200 years did not possess any religious sentiment[14] is to fly in the face of substantial evidence to the contrary. In the Rai document we are encountering the kind of visionary experience, though admittedly second-hand, similar to the one that Black Elk spoke of in his Great vision.[15]

The Rai enable men to see with an inner eye. This eye is a metaphysical gift akin to Grace or Nirvana, if not in its overall implications, then at least in terms of the qualitative identification between the man of high degree and the supra-mundane world. The initiate who has embarked upon the inward Dream Journey and participated in the ritual activity associated with various hot places or Dreaming sites, has, by his actions and involvement with tribal elders, entered into a metaphysical relationship with the Sky Heroes themselves. It is this relationship that so profoundly affects the entire Aboriginal culture even today, because through the Dream Journey all Aborigines are able to share in this principial bonding, each according to his or her nature and aptitude. Without the Dreaming, the Aboriginal culture would have disintegrated long ago. Their spiritual relationship with the land is not so much an end in itself as it is so often depicted by institutions and corporations eager to discount its authenticity. Because what these bodies consistently fail to recognize is the essential nature of this relationship and its role within the spiritual life of a traditional people whose theocentric pre-occupations take precedence over all other concerns. For the land, the hot places filled with *djang*, the mythological landscape that brings to bear a metaphysical perspective upon every outcrop and contour, the ritual invocation of spirit entities and the possibility of epiphanic identification that necessarily arises, these elements are at the root of an Aboriginal's love of his land. He or she does not love its materiality as such — although at times this love might be expressed in such terms because of the inadequacy of language — but instead what the land represents at a principial level. In the end, the land is no more than a bridge between himself and the sacred realm of the Dreaming.

The inward Dream Journey is the culmination of the cosmic pilgrimage. No Aborigine makes it unless he feels he is ready.

The route is littered with psychic terrors that have the power to destroy a man if he does not possess the inner certitude to resist. For this reason it is important to be under the guidance of a tribal elder or magician. Only these men know the barriers that exist barring entry into a full experience of the Dreaming. Ritual and hieratic song are thus important elements in a successful journey from one realm to another. But once the initiate has successfully made that journey he returns a different person. In the words of one informant, such a man returns as a 'spirit-of-the-dead'. "This puts him apart from others, it exalts this magician. They (the Rai) followed the 'aerial rope', that's the one they followed. They are spirits-of-the-dead, they don't walk on the ground. The world is big. They travel in the air following the 'aerial rope' all the time. Only magicians can see it. *He is a magician who follows the aerial rope all the time.*"[16] Thus only the man of high degree, the spiritualized man, can become totally identified with the Sky Heroes, in this case the Rai. It is he who has made the inward Dream Journey and returned as a dead man living, speaking the language of the Gods. And it is he who is at last in possession of that inner knowledge prized above all else by a race of people whose entire culture is dedicated to the sanctity of life. In the end, the Dream Journey is much more than a 'night-sea journey across paradisal waters'.[17] It is the beginning of a collusion between the man of high degree and the Spirit that made him.

Notes

1. W.E.H. Stanner, *Continuity and Change*. The Australian Journal of Science, 1958.

2. W.E.H. Stanner, *The Dreaming*. Australian Signpost, an Anthology, 1953.

3. A.P. Elkin, *Religion and Philosophy of the Australian Aborigines*. Essays in Honour of E.W. Thatcher.

4. C.P. Mountford, *Winbaraku and the Myth of Jarapiri*. 1968. Rigby.

5. Ibid.

6. Ibid.

7. A.P.Elkin, *Aboriginal Men of High Degree*, 1977. University of Queensland Press.

8. Ibid.

9. H.H.J. Coate, *The Rai and the Third Eye*. 1966. Oceania XXXVII.

10. Ibid. 'Wandjina is the important one. We say concerning him that he designed the world'.

11. A.P. Elkin, *Totemism in North-Western Australia*, Oceania Vol III, No. lv. 'They (the spirit entities known as Rai) live in the bush and wandering about at night are met by men in dreams.' cf. Jacob's dream, *Genesis 28:12*. 'And he dreamed, and behold a ladder set up on the earth, and the top of it reached to heaven: and behold the angels of God ascending and descending on it.'

12. cf. Wallis Budge, *The Book of Paradise I-II*, London 1904 p. 1004. Also C.-M. Edsman, Le bapteme de feu, p.155. We read here where the Egyptian Fathers recognized a monk who 'shone with the light of Grace'.

13. We are reminded here of a report on Saint Sabas being seen by the Emporor Justinian as 'a divine grace in the form of burning light...that radiated like the sun'. *Vita S. Sabae,* ed. E. Schwartz, p.173; J. Lemaitre, *Dictionnaire de Spiritualité*, 1952.

14. See previous chapter.

15. John G. Neihardt, *Black Elk speaks*. Pocket Books 1975.

16. Ibid.

17. C.G. Jung, *Symbols of Transformation*, p. 210.

CHAPTER 5
Nature as Numen

'He is seen in Nature in the wonder of a flash of lightning'
Kena Upanishad

It has often been noted that Aboriginal religious belief lacks the moral earnestness which we have come to expect of true religion. This is born out by the fact that Aboriginal religion is largely ritual and myth-based in its expression, devoid as it is of any formal theology to flesh out the mysteries that we find in so much of its poetry and songs. The idea of such soul-stirring statements as *Sanctus Dominus Deus Saboath* or 'Holy, Holy, Lord God Almighty' is entirely alien to the Aboriginal way of thinking. His religious outlook is not a conceptual formularization in the way of dogma, but instead is expressed as a vital force in everything that happens or is said or thought.

Thus to unravel the spiritual subtlety of an Aboriginal creation-myth or an erotic song-cycle requires us to dispense with certain prejudices as to what constitutes holiness or sanctity. Sometimes we have to reproduce in ourselves what Maurice Aniane called the 'cosmogenic unfolding' — that is, 'the permanent creation of the world in the sense in which all creation, finally, is only a Divine Imagination.'[1] In the process we begin to encounter what in Islamic esotericism is known as the *ta'wil*, a path by which we are 'lead back' via things, natural objects and sometimes scriptural exegesis from their outerness, or the letter, to their innerness or spirit. Aboriginal myths and stories require us to put aside our taste for moral amplification if we wish to penetrate the full depth of their meaning.

One myth that is capable of yielding the full depth of Aboriginal spirituality is associated with the Wadaman tribe and its sacred rain centre known as Wiyan Nalanjari. Located in a region some hundred kilometres west of Katherine in the

71

Northern Territory of Australia, this remote centre is made up of a series of caves, or rock-art galleries, that depict the story of two Lightning Brothers and a battle they wage in the sky at the beginning of each wet season. Jabiringi and Yagjagbula are the principal Sky Heroes of the Wadaman tribe, and as such feature as two spirit-beings painted in ochre on cave walls throughout the region.

Iconographically, both of the Lightning Brothers look very much alike. Their faces are made up of two eyes and a white, snake-like line originating at the nose that spirals in a uroboric fashion around the visage in a clock-wise direction to end at the mouth. Their heads are surrounded in a sun ray aureole with a central 'horn' protruding from the forehead; their bodies are made up of vertical ochred lines reaching to their feet (symbol of rain); and their mouths are linked by a red-ochre oesophagus to a giant phallus suspended between their legs that suggests a highly formalized expression of potency. The smaller of the two figures, that of Yagjagbula, is holding a stone axe in each hand. Only the older brother, Jabiringi, seems to be wearing what might be construed as wings sprouting from his shoulder-blades. The phallus on each figure has been sub-incised — a common practice among Aborigines of this region.

The overwhelming impression of anyone viewing the Lightning Brothers for the first time is one of wonder. Their eyes gaze down at you blindly, not unlike Greek statuary. Their expressions are those of spirit-beings in the grip of some awe-inspiring event. At the same time there is a powerful feeling of ritual potency that pervades the rock gallery at Yiwalalay. The fact that the phallus in turn is linked by a canal to the mouth of each brother reinforces the impression that both 'word' and 'semen' perfectly counterbalance one another. The ejaculatory Word of the Lightning Brothers is poised to impregnate the earth.

Nearby there is another site known as Ngalanjari ('Water Rock') which is important to Wadaman rain-making rituals. All these sites feature rock-art associated with various details pertaining to the myth of the Lightning Brothers. In the past, before the beginning of the wet season, these sites would have been visited by Wadaman tribesmen responsible for the performance of the rites. Here songs would have been sung and dances enacted to celebrate the anticipated re-appearance of the Lightning Brothers in the cloud-laden sky above. Each ritual was designed to re-affirm aspects of the myth in accordance with certain laws laid down at the time of the Dreaming. Nor were these laws created by men as such, but by the Sky Heroes themselves.

The myth of the Lightning Brothers can be paraphrased as follows: 'Rain came from the west, from a far country. It came towards Yinalari [Wadaman country] where, in the form of Rainbow Serpent [a rainbow], it descended. Rain was accompanied by the Lightning Brothers, Jabiringi and Yagjagbula who flashed and lit up the country from where they came. Rain meanwhile stopped at Yiwalalay, not far from Yinalari. Here the Lightning Brothers began fighting one another. Rainbow Serpent, too, shone in the darkened sky over Yiwalalay, refusing to remain for long over Yinalari.'

The story of 'Janininawuya' or the 'two lightnings' slowly evolves: 'The older Lightning Brother, Jabiringi, had a wife by the name of Ganayanda. She was his second wife and Yagjagbula was attracted to her. He decided to elope with her while Jabiringi was out hunting kangaroo one day. So, while Ganayanda was down at the waterhole gathering water, Yagjagbula abducted her. Meanwhile Jabiringi caught up with his younger brother and his wife. He confronted Yagjagbula and together they fought one another with boomerangs and nulla nullas [clubs]. While they fought the Frogs, which were journeying to Yinalari country along with Rain, stopped to observe the battle between the two lightnings. To mark the spot, the Frogs speared the nearby rock, causing clear water to flow forth. This spring is used by the Wadaman people for drinking even today. The Lightning Brothers continued to attack one another with boomerangs time after time. At last the older brother, Jabiringi, managed to hit the younger man on the head. When he threw his boomerang Jabiringi's blow caused the rock ['Water Rock'] to crack down the middle, as if it had split Yagjagbula's skull. Finally he managed to wrestle Yagjagbula's nulla nulla from him and toss it far away towards Barguya Creek. All the while Rain continued to fall while the Lightning Brothers fought. Such was the intensity of the battle that Rain began to wonder whether he had come all the way to Yinalari for nothing. So he moved on to Yiwalalay.'

The songman then interlocutes: 'The white crystals rising in the rock at 'Water Rock' Dreaming place has been produced by Rain. [This is calcite crystals being drawn up through the rock.] During the hot weather we only put a little water in the billy-can. But when the clouds 'throw' rain in the afternoon we have much more.'

The songman continues: 'The old men used to gather at Montejinnie where they would collect stones to pound the bark of the kapok bush. Then they would decorate their bodies and perform a rain-making corroboree. After that they would lie down and sleep for three days. On the fourth day the rain would invariably begin to fall. Clouds would build up while the Lightning Brothers would begin fighting. Then the rain would eventually stop and the Frogs fall silent. 'The real reason why those two brothers fought was that Jabiringi's wife, Ganayanda, belonged to the Yimbanari sub-section [presumably forbidden to him according to kinship laws. Or because his other wife, Gulidan, was of the Yimbalyari sub-section.]

'Anyway, Rainbow Snake continued to shine (or flash) at Jabiringu while he hung above Yinalari. Rain did not proceed beyond this point.'[2]

Thus we have a songman's rendition of the Lightning Brothers myth. On the surface we recognize a relatively simple story depicting the beginning of the wet season with rain-clouds drifting in from the Tanami Desert to the south-west, accompanied by lightning and rainbows. We observe natural phenomena anthropomorphized by the songman in order to support a mythological explanation of what is evidently a meteorological event. This is not unusual among traditional peoples when they choose to celebrate their kinship with nature. But what non-Aboriginal people mistakenly assume is that there is no metaphysical content to the story beyond some quasi-religious sentiment that might happen to accompany ritualistic observance.

If we are to understand the sacramental importance of the myth, we must listen firstly to one of the custodians of the 'Water Rock' site. Idumdum, or Bill Harney as he is more popularly known as, is responsible for the preservation of the Lightning Brothers and the various sites associated with the myth. It was he who first drew our attention to the cosmic battle that they perennially fight each wet season. While born and bred in Wadaman country, he has since crossed over into the European world. He now lives and works in Katherine. Although he has had a Christian upbringing, Bill Harney is in no doubt that his first allegiance is not to Jesus Christ but to his tribal spirit-beings, the Lightning Brothers. They are his avatars. It was he who explained further aspects of the iconography when we questioned him.

According to Bill, Jabiringu's extended phallus is a symbol of his *paraunda*, or power. As the more dominant Lightning Brother he is capable of ripping up trees and killing men instantly, particularly if they happen to be wearing metal pins in their hats or are caught carrying red meat across their shoulders. Jabiringu's *paraunda*, he suggests, is both a physical attribute as well as being symptomatic of a spiritual strength accorded to the spirit-being because of its status as a Dreaming figure. By thrusting his phallus deep in the ground (as a lightning discharge effectively does) Jabiringi is capable of 'fertilizing' the earth even as he uproots trees.

Yagjagbula, though a less dominant member of the duo, nevertheless possesses considerable *paraunda* of his own. According to Bill Harney the tiny axes that he carries are used 'to split trees' just as lightning is capable of doing. He too possesses a phallus of considerable potency, suggesting a capacity for impregnating the earth at the time of the wet season.

The two main protagonists in the cosmic drama are therefore clearly delineated. But there are others. The principal Aboriginal Sky Hero, Rainbow Snake, is present in his usual manifestation as a rainbow. He too has the capacity to 'flash', thus implying some sort of cosmic dialogue with the Lightning Brothers when they appear in the sky. Rain is also anthropomorphized as both a 'presence' and an observer. He is capable of observing the battle between the brothers while in part being responsible for it. It is as if Rain were, paradoxically, the feminine embodiment of the eloping wife, Ganayanda, since 'his' arrival precipitates the battle between the brothers. This male-female duality is not uncommon with regard to the rain-motif.[3]

The remaining participants in the drama are Frogs and men. The Frogs manage to contribute to the cosmic activity however when they spear the rocks to release clear water. The motif of spearing the earth in order to make it fruitful finds its parallel in the activities of the Persian Hero, Tishtriya[4], who takes the form of a white horse and splits open the rain-lake. Tishtriya is also known as Tir or 'arrow' and is sometimes represented as feminine, with a bow and arrow in his hand. According to a Mithraic text, Mithras shoots water from the rock with his arrow in order to stop the drought.[5] While accompanying Rain and observing the battle between the Lightning Brothers, it is evident that the Frogs contribute to the process of releasing life-giving waters onto the parched land, thus providing succour to the Wadaman people.

Men too are seen as contributing to the advent of rain. By re-creating the sacred decorations on their own bodies and performing the relevant dances before retiring to 'sleep' (meditate) for three days, they are seen as triggering a cloud-burst on the fourth day. Men are therefore drawn into the cosmic drama along with the Sky Heroes, and indeed are extremely important to its fulfillment.

Yet if we look at the Lightning Brothers myth in its universal sense we see more than a rain-increase story. Clearly the Lightning Brothers represent much more to the Wadaman people than a couple of spirit-beings with an ambivalently malign aspect to their natures who happen to get into a fight over a woman. The hagiography alone suggests links with material found in myths from other ancient cultures. The Cain-Abel conflict comes to mind, as does the wrestling match between the soul-brothers, Gilgamesh and Enkidu, in the 3000 year-old Sumerian epic. But more significantly to our present investigation is the Arthurian story of the two warring brothers, Balin and Balan, described by Thomas Malory.[6]

In the story, Balin earns the ire of a certain damsel when he refuses to give back her a fairy sword that he has managed to draw from an intractable sheath. She warns him, "You are not wise to keep the sword from me; for you shall slay with the sword the best friend that ye have, and the man that you most love in the world, and the sword shall be your destruction." After numerous adventures in which Balin, in spite of his good intentions, manages to wreak havoc wherever he goes, the younger brother eventually encounters on the field of battle his own brother, Balan, 'the man he most loved in the world' whose destruction the fairy maiden had prophesized. Balan at this time was the priest and guardian of the Woman's Isle and thus the protector of the Sanctuary of Life. Not able to recognize his brother in his armour because Balin had sacrificed his heraldic shield for that of another, Balan fought Balin to the death. 'And so they aventyrd their spears and came marvelously fast together, and they smote each other in the shields . . .' Since they were of similar strength, and two aspects of the same being, they fought until they were out of breath and the ground about them was a river of blood.

The final encounter between the two brothers runs as follows: 'Then they went to battle again so marvelously that doubt it was to hear of that battle for the great blood-shedding, and their hauberks unnailed, that naked they were on every side. At last Balan the younger brother withdrew him a little and laid him down. Then said Balin The Savage, "What knight are thou? For or now I found never so knight that matched me."

'"My name is," said he, "Balan, brother unto the good knight Balin."

'"Alas," said Balin, "that ever I should see this day," and therewith he fell backward in a swoon.'

The parallels between this tale and the much older material imbedded in the Lightning Brothers myth are obvious. Two brothers, one older and one younger, do battle over a theft inspired by a woman. That both pairs of siblings lay one another low implies the neutralization of those destructive forces unleashed by their mutual antagonism. Their war with one another is a fight to the death. Yet in destroying each other and laying low the two sides of the same 'sundered personality'[7] (as suggested by their kinship), they are able to become reconciled. In the case of the Lightning Brothers, this reconciliation finds its expression in the commencement of the wet season and the influx of those life-giving waters so necessary to the survival of the Wadaman people.

Yagjagbula's actions in wanting to defend his wife who has been abducted 'from the waterhole' finds echoes in the Balan-Balin story. At the time of their encounter Balan occupied the role of defender of the Isle of Woman and the protector of the Sanctuary of Life. Ganayanda's persona as the female principle, the universal womb or Sanctuary of Life clearly requires her husband to get her back, to 'protect' her, whatever her motives might have been at the time of the abduction.

The same conflicting motives are present at the time of Helen's elopement with Paris to Troy. In spite of being cuckolded, Menelaus still felt it necessary to reclaim Helen as his own because she represented much more to him and the people of Hellas than the scarlet woman. For, although a supremely seductive figure (like Ganayanda?), Helen is nevertheless a fragmentary aspect of the Great Mother, the beloved, the very womb of life. Ganayanda's questionable loyalty to her husband and her seduction of Yagjabula is consistent with the Great Mother's overpowering capacity for love — a capacity that drives men like Paris to abuse the laws of hospitality while a guest in Menelaus' palace, and forces Yagjagbula to justify his own actions by invoking the rather flimsy excuse of broken kinship taboos. In both cases we see Man as victim; but a victim of the terrible instinctive force of love which destroys (the fall of Troy, the Lightning Brothers' battle) before the redemptive process can begin.

When we consider the weapons carried by the Lightning Brothers it is clear that their sacred origins are separate from their actual manifestation. While lightning bolts are the result of electrical discharges into the atmosphere, they are also the sceptres of kingship, the divine thyrsus of the gods. In an Orphic Hymn to Zeus, the most powerful god in the Greek pantheon, we are informed that 'Zeus was first and Zeus last, he with the glittering lightnings . . ... Zeus is king, Zeus is the ruler of all things, he with the gleaming lightnings'. Homer continually refers to Zeus by his surname *nephelegeretes*, which means that he was the god who 'assembled clouds'. He was also known as the 'Rain God' and the god of 'Lightning', all of which preserves his quality as the 'god of weather'.[8] The battle between Jabiringi and Yagjagbula is in its own way a genuine clash of Titans, both of whom aspire to divinity as weather-gods. They, like Zeus, embody a certain primevil *paraunda* or *puissance* that sets them apart from other culture-heroes such as Rain or even the Rainbow Snake itself.

There is a further parallel with the Zeus myth in the story of the god's marriage to one of his daughters, Demeter (the Barley Goddess). Yagjagbula's abduction of Ganayanda because she was of the wrong kinship group is in line with the incest motif as suggested by Zeus' relationship with his daughter. We also note that in Aboriginal society women were traditionally the gatherers of leguminous foodstuffs in the same way that Demeter was responsible for the harvest. Demeter herself was known to have taken a lover whom she had laid with in a 'thrice-ploughed' field. From this union was born the child Ploutos ('Wealth'), and the earth subsequently brought forth an abundant harvest.[9] Zeus finally killed her lover with his lightning — in the same way as Jabiringi attempted to do away with his own brother. The significance of the two brothers doing battle with the aid of lightning in order to bring on the rain (wealth) is clearly evident.

This does not mean that there is any direct link whatsoever between the myth material of ancient Greece, or indeed of Celtic Europe, and that of the Wadaman people. All that is suggested here is that there are distinct parallels at work among the various traditions which only serve to underline these themes for what they are — the universal expressions of complex metaphysical ideas that in themselves point towards a profound spiritual legacy not present in more secular tales. The fact that the actions of Zeus, 'The Father', are analogic to earlier myth material found in such ancient cultures as the Australian Aborigines only serves to highlight the primordial nature of divine events wherever — and however — they manifest themselves.

This link extends to the Rainbow Serpent itself. Known as 'Pulwaiya' (lit. Father's Father) and long accepted as the most potent expression of Deity among Aborigines throughout the continent, the Rainbow Snake not only commanded thunder and lightning (therefore orchestrating the commencement of the wet season), it was also regarded as the maker of rivers and the builder of the road along which the pre-existent spirit-child enters its mother's womb.[10] The link between the Rainbow Serpent and the Lightning Brothers is further emphasized by a Hopi Indian belief which states that snakes are at the same time flashes of lightning auguring rain. When one considers a more recent commentator, Jacob Boehme, who regarded lightning as signifying a sudden rapture or illumination, then we begin to see the connection between the Rainbow Snake as a cult-figure and its role within Aboriginal tradition as the Truth-revealer.

This is further emphasized by a number of important details. The rainbow itself is no ordinary manifestation, but a bridge over which only gods can walk in safety. For a man to attempt such a journey would immediatly result in his death. Unlike gods, he must pass 'under' it. Indeed, among Aborigines, the only man capable of making this ascent is a *karadji* or clever-man. He alone can take up a postulant on the rainbow in order that the man might receive the inner knowledge known only to the Rainbow Serpent. In North-Western Australia, for example, a *karadji* took up a postulant via the rainbow in the following manner. Assuming the form of a skeleton, he placed the postulant into a pouch about his waist. At this stage the postulant has already been reduced to the size of a child by an act of magic. Then, sitting astride the rainbow, the *karadji* pulled himself up the rainbow hand over hand. Nearing the top, he threw the young man, now no more than a homunculus, out over the sky where the young man lay as if 'dead'. The *karadji* finally inserted into the inert body of the postulant some rainbow-snakes and quartz crystals, themselves scintillas of the divine radiance, as part of the initiatory process.

After this initial journey up the rainbow the postulant returned to earth with his guide and received more injections of quartz crystals. He was then allowed to 'wake up' — that is, come out of the trance under which he has been for the duration of the ceremony. In time the young postulant was able to make the journey up the rainbow alone so as to receive further instruction in his profession.

Such a journey across the rainbow-bridge to the land of the Sky Heroes implies an other-worldly dimension to the Rainbow Snake's character. It is not simply the upwelling of primordial anxieties implied by the snake's contrasting nature as the Mistress of Earth and the Underworld that we find when

81

it adopts the uroboric form of the Mother Goddess. This is only another side of the Rainbow Snake's character which serves to affirm the metaphysical ambivalence of the Sky Hero as a true numen or spirit. More importantly, perhaps, the journey up the rainbow signifies the gap that exists between Man and the spirit-world of the Dreaming. Only those men who have transcended the conditional world of manifestation are capable of making this trek into the otherworld, and then only when they have been reduced once more to a state of child-like innocence.

The uroboric nature of the Rainbow Snake is always present, however. Just as the dragon, or serpent, dwells in caverns and dark places, it nevertheless needs to be overcome if we are to conquer our lower self and achieve a level of wholeness. Zeus himself was known by the epithet *chthonios* or 'of the dark depths' and invariably appeared as a serpent. In the visage of Jabiringi we see this ancient image of the self-fecundating primal god permanently expressed: the uroborus joins the nose (orifice of inhaling and therefore of 'inspiration') with that of the mouth (through which the primal Word is expressed). It is clear that the Wadaman painters when they first depicted the Lightning Brothers on the cave walls were grappling with how best to image the 'self-manifesting' and 'self-expressing' god.

The inhalation of the Spirit or 'breath of life' and its subsequent expulsion as the Creative Word or Principle is an ancient motif found in both Egyptian and Hindu mythology alike. St John's injunction that 'the Word was God' further enhances the semenal nature of deity. That the Wadaman painters chose to express this awful truth by joining the nose to the mouth to the phallus once more highlights the fructive essence contained within the essential nature of the Lightning Brothers themselves. They are not simply primitive mythological figures, but early icons of deity as embodied in the Rainbow Snake itself.

What the Lightning Brothers encapsulate is the complex

and often contradictory nature of the Rainbow Snake. According to Orphic terminology, for example, the etymology of the name of the half-man, half-god and warrior, Heracles, means the 'coiling snake' and as such represents the zodiacal path of the sun. The Rainbow Snake's perennial return to Wadaman country at the time of the wet season in the form of a rainbow, itself created from the refracted light of the sun through water, is also an expression of the fulfillment of the zodiacal cycle. The Rainbow Snake's presence at the divine battle between the two warrior brothers helps to define the cosmic relevance of their encounter. They are not embittered siblings as such, but protagonists of a supra-mundane order celebrating the regenerative power of water — a power embodied in Ganayanda, the 'water-carrier' herself. The Rainbow Snake and rain are, therefore, inextricably entwined; the catalyst for their manifestation is the battle between the Lightning Brothers after Ganayanda's abduction while she was down at the waterhole 'looking for water'.

The Lightning Brothers myth is none other than the sanctification of certain natural phenomena. It was Thales who said that 'the Gods are in everything'. The Wadaman songmen have created a myth that affirms this principle. Nature, as far as they are concerned, obeys laws without deviation. They see in these natural events the character of their Causes, all of which draws them closer to the mysterious realm of the Dreaming. Celebrating the battle between the Lightning Brothers allows them to actively participate in the cosmic drama rather than remain merely as observers only. To cross the Rainbow-bridge and enter into the full mystery of creation is not simply a millennial hope with little prospect of realization. The Wadaman songmen know that such a journey is possible since the idea has always been a central tenet of their spiritual life. They know that the uroboric visage of Jabiringi and Yagjagbula is none other than a manifestation of the sacred labyrinth leading to the inner sanctuary of the Rainbow Snake. Bill Harney informed us that one of the important acts in the rain-making ceremony was to draw a stone knife through the sub-incised penis of the figures painted on the walls. This, he told us, was to Cut Old Man Rain and make him bleed. In such a sympathetic act of magic it was hoped to draw forth from the Sky Hero's phallus the procreative fluid stored up over the period of the dry season. Rain, the regenerative gift of the Sky Heroes, the perennial font of baptism into which the land must be immersed if it is to be renewed, becomes at last the Frogs' spears (rain, after all, is 'thrown') thus releasing those life-giving waters upon Wadaman country once more. This is presented as the blood pouring forth from the gods as they bleed for his people as intimated by Bill Harney when he 'cuts Old Man Rain to make him bleed'. While we see no connection here with the Eucharist, nonetheless the symbolism is obvious. The God-man, Jesus Christ, bled in order that men might be saved. So too does the Rainbow Snake through his avatars, Jabiringi and Yagjagbula, bleeds for his beloved Wadaman people.

The Lightning Brothers myth is therefore much more than a rain-increase story. To treat it as such would be to denigrate the metaphysical world-view inherent in the battle between these Sky Heroes. Indeed every religion and every world-view is entitled to be judged, not by the levels to which it is flattened, or coursened, but by the summits and pinnacles to which it aspires. From the Aboriginal point of view the myth of the Lightning Brothers embodied complex metaphysical data that gives real spiritual credance to re-occurring natural phenomena. Rain is the source of life for the Wadaman people. The fact that it is accompanied by thunder and lightning only serves to exaggerate the cosmic disturbance that they expect to witness at the end of each dry season.

Nevertheless, the threat that the rains might not come always remains. While observation has taught the Wadaman people to recognize the signs that the wet season is about to begin, they also know that if Jabiringi does not fight his brother for the re-possession of Ganayanda, then there is every chance that the Frogs will not throw their spears or Rainbow Snake flash his tongue. This is the crux of what becomes a genuine metaphysical dilemma for the Wadaman people. It also forms the basis of all ritual observance, whether these rituals involve recitations as every Station of the Cross, or they involve the phallus being 'cut until Old Man Rain bleeds'. In each case the act of benison is designed to cleanse a man's soul even as he performs the rites.

The Lightning Brothers are true avatars. Their field of battle however is as much the human soul as the air above Wadaman country. Significantly, the single horn protruding from their foreheads and their sun-like aureoles denote their majesty. According to the early Christian commentator, Priscillian, God was 'one-horned'[11] and therefore unique. Alexander, when deified, was often portrayed with ram's horns protruding from his temples as a symbol of his solar status. This archetypal image is further enhanced by Hippolytus who likens the serpent to the one-horned bull when he says: 'They say, too, that all things are subject to her [the serpent], that she is good and *has something of everything* in herself [our italics] as the horn of the one-horned bull. She imparts beauty and ripeness to all things . . .'. Again we can see yet another example of the primordial link between the Lightning Brothers and the Rainbow Snake. Clearly they are its precursor in the process of re-establishing cosmic order, since 'The horn that glistens yonder like a roof with four wings sides, with that do we drive out kshetriya hereditory disease from thy limbs,' as it is said in one of the hymns from the Atharva-Veda (III,7).

So that the Lightning Brothers, by their actions, signify the positive nature of mutual self-destruction in the interests of cosmic renewal. This is the basis of a profound spiritual truth and one that is not lost on the Wadaman people. The Sky Heroes' battle cannot be in vain since in doing so they are able to impart to the Wadaman people knowledge of the 'beauty and ripeness to all things' that comes with the advent of the wet season. Here we are dealing with that primordial encounter between the Spirit and its material manifestation on the one hand, and Man's recognition of that event on the other. Both of these are acknowledged by all religious systems and world-views whether they be montheistic, polytheistic or animistic in temper.

It is not surprising then that the Lightning Brothers are so revered by the Wadaman people. Not only do they represent an important numen for them, but they also help to preserve their cultural identity in a vast and lonely Eden. Yet they are important to non-Aborigines as well. For we see in them prototypes of our own divine representations which are no more or less 'primitive' simply because we might choose to express them in different ways. Indeed the Wadaman people give us insight into mankind's constant endeavour to realize the shape of divinity in all its mysterious and subtle forms. These one-horned rain-gods embrace a vision of beauty and renewal that is capable of haunting us even as we step back among the arid tumulae of our own de-mythologized landscape.

Notes

1. *Material for thought*, Maurice Aniane. Spring 1976.
2. *Wadaman Mythology Associated with Delamere Sites*, Francesca Merlan. Ms only.
3. *Symbols of Transformation*, C.G. Jung. Routledge & Kegan Paul. pp 289.
4. *Song of Tishtriya*.
5. *Textes*, pp136, Franz Cumont.
6. *Le Morte D'Arthur*, Sir Thomas Malory. Book II. Penguin Books.
7. *The King and the Corpse*, Hienrich Zimmer. pp 148.
8. *The Gods of the Greeks*, C Kerényi. pp116. Thames & Husdson.
9. Ibid.
10. *The Australian Aborigines*, A.P. Elkin. pp 256.
11. 'Unicornis est Deus' (One-horned is God).

CHAPTER 6
The Metaphysics of Space

It has been suggested that nomadic peoples, because of their indifference to a settled mode of existence, lack any fixed metaphysical perspective. Their pantheon of spirit-beings, their djinns and goblins, are often regarded as symptomatic of an uncentred or shifting spiritual viewpoint in keeping with the nomad's hunger for movement. Whether he is a Tuareg, a Sioux Indian or an Anatolian gypsy, the nomad is looked upon as someone who refuses to be confined by dogmatic belief, since it might restrict his ability to survive in any one place.

As a nomadic people the Australian Aborigines have suffered a great deal at the hands of their more sedentary European neighbours. European land ownership and the rush to portion the continent into vast agricultural allotments have seen the demise of the true nomadic Aborigine in the last one hundred years. Except for a few isolated pockets in the Central Desert region, there is now little evidence of any tribal movements among indiginous Aborigines as of old. The nomadic Aborigine has become land-locked in mission ghettoes or reservations left over from a time when both Church and State were the servile instruments of land-owners and the stock industry.

Yet it was the Aborigine's understanding of space, his ability to establish for himself a sense of 'place' while in a state of wandering, that gave him his unique human and spiritual dimension. Unlike the sederunt — that is, the person conditioned to living in one place — the Aborigine lives within the realm of 'the swift-perishing, never-to-be-repeated moment'[1] Over countless millenia he has learnt to glory in these fleeting moments and the presence of the eternal that lies within the harmonious interplay of daily impressions and experiences.

Thus we are confronted with a perception of space that is

non-architectural, non-mathematical and indeed non-material when it is detached from the actuality of the land itself. For the country or tribal territory over which a clan is entitled to move is a symbolic landscape contingent on supernatural, not physical events that might have occurred in the past. These supernatural events have occurred outside time during that eternal moment known in Aboriginal cosmology as the Dreaming. It is for this reason that we can refer to the non-material aspect of the land, given that its physical presence is of a lower order to that of its *meta*-physical condition.

The very nature of non-architectural or non-mathematical space for the sederunt is one of concern, even conflict. To live in a space that is not defined in some way offers the prospect of inhabiting a region of wilderness, or worse — a wasteland. The cultural history of sedentary peoples is one of confronting the idea of wilderness and taming it so that it conforms to defined canons of measure. These canons may have a metaphysical significance, such as in the construction of the city of Ecbatan in Medea which, according to Herodotus, was surrounded by seven concentric walls each of a different colour signifying the seven planets, with the treasury located in its citadel or sacred centre. Ulug Beg, the 15th Century Mongol king also attempted to model his capital, Samarkand, so that it might reflect the celestial order of the heavens.

Thus the town or social centre was regarded as a contrived universe. It either represented a supermundane principle as in the case of Ecbatan, or it became a bastion against the threat posed by wilderness as in the case of the brush fence about an African kraal. In both these examples, however, lay an attempt to impose order upon what was inherently *dis*ordered by a people who regarded 'chaos', or the formlessness of the environment, as a profoundly negative condition. Sedentary peoples are afraid of wilderness precisely because it signifies an un 'civilised' state — that is, a state where the individual is deprived of the virtue of citizenship and thereby becomes diminished as a person in consequence.

The Aborigine's penchant for space, for movement, for the nomadic lifestyle is inspired, of course, by his need to survive. The slender resources of the environment make it imperative that he move from one place to another in order to discover new points of abundance. But beyond that, he is in the grip of a far greater imperative that urges him to pursue his life as a nomad. As far as the nomad is concerned, what the sederunt might regard as a hostile and forbidding wilderness is for him an imperishable wonderland of images that serve to define his spiritual existence. Unlike the sederunt, who is at the mercy of numbers and of enclosed space, the nomad lives in a world of openness which is only conscribed by the limitations of the imagination itself.

Social space for the Aborigine is therefore arbitary. He is able to construct a camping ground or a ritual site simply by arranging a few stones or building shelters sufficient for the needs of the clan during its stay. These in turn can 'disappear' when their usefullness has been exhausted. There is no allegiance displayed towards the composed environment once it has served its purpose. This non-materialist approach to objects, be they composed of 'place' or simply as utile artifacts, is another cause for suspicion among sederunts. The idea that things should only be 'possessed' for a limited duration suggests a non-economic world-view at odds with sedentary ideals. Ultimately, it is this world-view that most threatens the life of the sederunt. His insistence on ownership, on legal possession is undermined by the nomad's dismissal of such values.

On the other hand the Aborigine prefers a lack of clear definition when it comes to defining social space. He is content to feel it with his own body rather than rely on the existence of formal boundaries. As Big Bill Neidjie, a Kakadu Aborigine, says, 'I feel it with my body, with my blood. Feeling all these trees, all this country . . .. When the wind blows you can feel it. Same for country . . .. You feel it. You can look, but feeling . . .. that make you. *Out there in open space*' (our italics)[2]. Clearly a level of intellectual fluidity conditions the way the Aborigine approaches his environment. He is loathe to announce its boundaries. He is reluctant to give it a formal dimension except as an extension to his own being. As far as he is concerned, the land, the space in which he moves and finds his spiritual reality, can only 'come through his body'.

Such a view contrasts strongly with the sederunt's perception of his environment. For a sedentary person, his environment is an objective reality that has been created out of his own imagination. A cathedral, a mosque, even a house or a village-square are the objective representations of inner ideals. For the nomad, and in particular the Aborigine, the reverse is true. He sees the physical environment as a projection of the architypes that govern his existence, real or imaginary. Thus he is able to imbue this landscape with values that the sederunt might consider at best pantheistic, or at worst superstitious.

Further, we find that the Aborigine's relationship to the space he occupies is reflected in his actions. Since his space is not constricted by numbers nor by the idea of time, he is able to adopt an entirely different posture, both at an intellectual and physical level. When he is in a state of repose or when he is engaged in action, his body is perfectly adapted to spaciousness. Aborigines rarely sit down close to one another; in fact, when they do come together to talk, they invariably sit about with a great deal of space between them. It is as if they wish to preserve a feeling of 'distance' in keeping with their understanding of its limitlessness. So we are confronted with a definite 'rhythm' in the posture of the nomad, whether he is walking, running, committed to some ritual action or sitting quietly on the ground.

It is this idea of carrying unlimited space within the physical actions of the body that gives the Aborigine his particular identity. His body is as much a reflection of the land that he calls his own as a demonstration of his physical prowess or athletic ability. The way he moves his limbs, his easy agility that on the surface may appear to be almost lethargic — these manifestations serve to identify the individual for who he is. Unlike the sederunt, the nomad carries his whole world within himself. He does not need to rely on outward exigencies to define his personality. His world is almost entirely devoid of visual icons; and when they do present themselves they are almost always depicted in a highly stylized or abstract fashion.

Clothing is another unimportant accoutrement for the Aborigine. It is assumed by many that Australia is either so hot, or that Aborigines are so tough that they have no requirement for clothing. Neither of these assumptions are true. Australia can be very cold in winter, even in desert regions. The need to wear clothing often stems from a desire for privacy, particularly among sedentary peoples. Since their space is so confined, they must 'conceal' themselves behind a barrier of clothing in order to preserve this privacy. Religious and sexual taboos are also preserved by the use of clothing. Concealing the body is one way of protecting the inner man. But for the Aborigine, clothing his body quickly destroys the relationship he enjoys with his land, with his 'space', since it separates him from what he is. It is significant in this respect to observe how Adam, after the loss of his innocence, recognized his nakedness and hid from the sight of God.[3] When he quit the Garden of Eden he was wearing a 'coat of skins' given to him by God.

This lack of concern for apparel by Aborigines signifies a high level of un-selfconsciousness. For sedentary peoples such as the first European invaders of Australia, this primordial 'innocence' was regarded as an extreme example of their primitivity. The very fact that nomadic Australians did not wear clothes worked against them in the estimation of Europeans. They were regarded as being little more than animals since they had made no attempt to separate themselves from nature. Indeed it was this hiatus between man and nature that Europeans regarded as the epitome of the civilized being. The further man distanced himself from his primordial condition, the more acutely aware he became of his self- consciousness. It was this quality of sophistication, this dandyfication, that made it possible for the European mind to measure the humanity of the nomadic Aborigines during their early period of contact with absolute impunity. Clothing, or lack of it, became an important yardstick because it served to identify personality, material status, vocation, even eccentricity to the European. A naked man, therefore, was a non-person in view of his refusal to conform to the accepted mode of covering up the body.

It is not surprising then that when Aborigines were rounded up in the latter part of the 19th century, the first thing that was demanded of them was to wear clothing. This was the first step in a programme of 'de-nomadizing' them. By making them aware of their bodies as a thing separate from nature, by instructing them in the art of self-consciousness, it was hoped that Aborigines would give up their nomadic ways. Going on 'walkabout' was discouraged, also, not only by mission chaplains but by graziers who had learnt to exploit their talent as stockmen. It became clear to the grazier that going on walkabout was uneconomic and needed to be suppressed as a cultural activity. The issuing of clothing, blankets, flour and sugar were all important elements in the process of sedentizing the nomad.

Such a policy had proved very successful among North American Indians. At the time of the Indian Wars, tribesmen who submitted to the invading US Army were immediately stripped of their traditional costumes and forbidden to live in round-shaped teepees. Instead they were condemned to wearing European clothing and forced to live in 'square' houses, which in time lead to their extinction as nomad cultures. It is said that these square houses directly contributed to the epidemic of tuberculosis that decimated many of the Plains tribes after their defeat at Wounded Knee in 1890.

Furthermore, what apparel or decoration that the nomadic Aborigine resorted to was in keeping with the fullness of his identity and his environment. A G-string of skin cord and leaves, a plaited split cane armlet and a head-band made from plaited hair that served to 'crown' the head — these were considered sufficient covering for a warrior. His principal accoutrements, however, were not his slender range of apparel or even his weapons. Indeed the fullness of his being both as an individual and as a clan citizen, was reflected in the totemic scars on his body. These ritual patterns distinguished him in the eyes of his fellow clansmen. More importantly, perhaps, they distinguished the man in the eyes of his totemic spirits. His ipseity was fully determined by these markings, but in a way that was in keeping with the 'markings' of his own country.

It is significant that Aboriginal clothing, what little there is of it, reflects the uncluttered nature of the landscape itself. For much of the Australian continent is clothed with a sparce layer of flora. Tall stands of trees are rare except in tropical enclaves. In contrast, much of the continent is clothed in low scrub, open grasslands and an abundance of native wildflowers in a good season. These wildflowers, as exotic as they appear among the parched brownness of the rest of the country, are as vivid as tribal markings on a man's chest. Even a watercourse in the desert, dry for most of the year, clearly 'marks' the landscape like a cicatrice by way of the gum trees that line its banks.

Indeed it is ritual clothing that determines the nomadic Aborigine's cultural integration into the world that he knows. Body decoration and scarification are an important register of social development among these people. They are used to celebrate the passage rites of Aborigines from birth when the new-born babies are painted white, a decoration usually continued throughout the suckling period. From this point onward, the body becomes a veritable religious icon whereby temporary and permanent decorations mark changes in status of the individual under the aegus of religious ceremony.[4]

At puberty, for example, the girl is ceremonially 'made' into a woman, accompanied by body decoration and special hairstyles. The girl then retires to a secluded part of the camp with female relatives, who teach her the taboos associated with menstruation, as well as details on the clan's moral and spiritual outlook. She is richly decorated and acclaimed by other members of the clan as an adult woman. On Melville Island near Darwin, the girl is painted red and yellow by her father. He also dresses her hair, building it up into a mop by twisting the curled strands of human hair on top of a bamboo chaplet, attached to which is an ornament of flattened dogs' tails set in beeswax.[5]

These decorations, which in themselves are sacred 'clothing', clearly make the Aborigine into a living icon. Since the designs are generally of a sacred origin, being conventionalized representations of the clan country and its mythology, they transcend the secular condition of pure decoration to become embodiments of both the land's sanctity and the Dreaming spirits that created the land in the first place. These patterns are the sole property of clan members and are commonly inherited from the father. The Aborigine's hereditary clan design is very important to the individual. Indeed it is regarded with considerable reverence as it embodies a part of his spirit. In this respect blood feuds of the past were often the result of a mark of disrespect shown towards a clan's designs or the theft of the pattern itself. Furthermore, the clan design was not the inherited possession of the living only. A dead man's skull usually reflected his clan's motifs long after the burial rituals had been concluded.

So body decoration is an important form of clothing for Aborigines. Not only does it declare a man's (or woman's) identity, both as an individual and a member of a clan, it reaffirms his (or her) relationship with the sacred nature of the clan's country. In this respect, the decorations become a representation of the land on or 'in' the being of that person. Resorting to the land as camouflage reinforces this idea of oneness. As an example, kangaroo hunters disguise themselves with blue earth in the mud-flats and with red ochre in the laterite regions of the country. In this way they resort to clothing themselves with their own country as a way of deceiving their prey.

Tribal games, too, often reflect clan territory in a particular way. Janjula women of the Gulf Country, for example, are adept at using string for their entertainment. They are capable of making elaborate string patterns using their hands and even their feet. They are also capable of making representations of different animals and objects familiar to them from their wanderings about their country. Eaglehawks, possums, lizards and canoes are popular among the Janjula women. It sometimes takes more than one woman to construct a dugong, say, using a separate piece of string each. It is clear, however, that these string games reflect the world outside — that is, the world they encounter during their nomadic wanderings.

Further evidence of the Aborigine's unique ability to delineate space as a metaphysical entitiy is outlined in dance ceremonies. Among all traditional peoples it is common to regard the act of dancing in its ceremonial and entertainment context only. Clan totem dances, or dances that reiterate Dreaming events, rain-dances or dances designed to encourage a successful conclusion to the hunt, these are seen in terms of the story they wish to portray and the efficacy of their results. But there is another important aspect of the dance that becomes a method of spatial expression par excellence. Because it is in the dance that the Aborigine best expresses his commitment to nomadism. Unlike sedentary peoples who rely on their entire body, particularly their hands and face (as in South-East Asian dancing), the Aborigine relies for his principal effect upon his feet and legs — the very limbs that carry him across his own country.

The driving rhythm of a dancer's feet as he pummels the ground is a special feature of Aboriginal performance. At the same time the legs are always bent, so that the dancer appears to his audience in a crouching position, as if he were stalking an animal in the wild. The rythmic beating of the ground in turn provokes a drum-like response, thus drawing the earth into a dialogue with the dancer. In a ceremonial context the dancer is striving to hear some 'echo' from the earth that affirms the

physical articulation of the mythic or religious material he is
endeavouring to express.

To the observer the dance soon becomes a ceremonial
interplay between the dancer and his earth. The presence of
body decorations and head-dresses merely heighten what is
already a joining together of the dancer with the mythic
material that has been created out of the wilderness beyond the
edge of the dance site. In this way the wilderness so abhorrant
to the sederunt is drawn into the ritual world of the nomad
where it is celebrated. The so-called 'wildness' of the primevil
landscape is in turn passified, becoming by a process of
ritualization an active participant in the cosmic pageant
embodied in the dance itself. It is at this point that the dance
becomes a symbolic representation of space, the space that
conscribes the Aboriginal nomad in both a geologic and
anthropomorphic fashion. In the words of a Gagadju tribesman
when he gazed out over the floodplain in his clan territory,
"This earth, she my mother."

Indeed, for the Aboriginal nomad, the land is a kind of
palimsest. On its worn and rugged countenance he is able to
write down the great stories of Creation, his creation, in such a
way as to insure their renewal. Walking from one sacred spot to
another, performing rituals that have changed little over the
millenia, are in themselves important aspects of a metaphysical
dialogue. Since Aboriginal society is pre-literate, this dialogue
relies on intellectual and imaginative contact with sacred
constructs within the landscape that have been invested with
miwi, or power, according to tradition or the Law. The
language, of course, is one of symbolic expression, of mythic
reportage. The *miwi* or power associated with a sacred spot is
revealed to the individual when he is prepared to engage in an
act of contemplation, in what Cicero termed *cognito contem-
platioque naturae*. Thus the Aboriginal nomad's encounter with
the spatial aspect of landscape becomes a meditative act rather
than a physical one. To the Aborigine his country is the very
embodiment of tradition.

The words of a Juki gypsy from central Asia reflect a similar viewpoint when he speaks of his own tradition. 'Our tradition is not in archives or documents. Tradition is like spring-water that wells forth from the ground, flowing on forever. It is no abstract doctrine; it is respect for the harmony woven into all things. Tradition is not the butterfly you have killed and placed under glass; it is in the living voice of life itself, forever free to expand and develop. Tradition means to pursue fullness and let your eyes be glutted with honey. The ancient wellsprings of the past have not died, but remain here, within us, and nourish our warm desires. Even the desert rose grows better when it receives special attention. We are privileged to be here, where the tradition has fermented for many generations. But if you leave this place, you will find that it has not left you.'[6]

When we compare these remarks with Bill Neidjie, we hear similar conclusions: 'When that law started? I don't know how many thousands of years ago. Europeans say 40,000 years, but I reckon myself probably was more because . . . it is sacred. Rock stays, earth stays. I die and put my bones in cave or earth. Soon my bones become earth . . . [they become] all the same. My spirit has gone back to my country. We always use what we got . . . old people and me. I look after my country, now lily coming back. Lily, nuts, birds, fish . . .. whole lot coming back. We got to look after everything, can't waste anything. Old people tell me, "You got to keep law [tradition]." "What for?" I said. "No matter we die but that law . . . you got to keep it. You can't break law. Law must stay." '[7]

It is clear that nomadic peoples, whoever they might be, view their country in a similar fashion. But because these societies are largely pre-literate there is a tendency to regard the landscape as an embodiment of the Sacred Word. In order to read it's spiritual message it becomes necessary for the nomad to regularly traverse his tribal territory, just as a devout sederunt might observe the liturgical cycle associated with his spiritual discipline each time he attends mosque or church.

In music and singing there is further evidence of the

Aborigine's reverence for space. Aboriginal instruments are confined to the boomerang, clapsticks and didgeridoo. All these instruments are made from carved or hollowed-out wood. Aborigines possess no stringed instruments, drums or flutes. The range of sound these instruments of theirs make is very low, in keeping with the normal sounds they hear about them. Nature, it seems, is the tuning-fork that Aborigines listen to when they are playing or singing a song. They do not strive after shrillness or cacophany as we hear among many other more strident cultures. The idea of formal scales is foreign to them, not because they are not capable of perceiving tonal or pitch difference, but because the range of emotions that they wish to express in music is far narrower. The extreme emotionalism that characterizes Western secular music is not what they desire to achieve. Singing, indeed the song as a metaphysical entity, is a product not of an individual but of tradition. Since it is handed down to them from the Dreaming, the song has a sacred life independant of those that sing it, and those who listen.

The reality of a song and its mode of expression is therefore profoundly interrelated. Songs are 'owned' by different skin groups within the clan. To try and steal a song from someone is an act of desecration and can often lead to blood feuds. Ownership, in fact, can only be transferred to a younger sibling at death, or inherited at birth by all new members of a particular skin group.[8]

Teaching a song is a formal activity that requires concentrating on accurate performance of melody, rhythm, accompaniment and texts. This stage is only the first part of the process of progressive revelation. During later stages, explanations of the associated myths, texts, ceremonial objects and accompanying rituals is more fully detailed. Teaching is normally done by the owner of the song-cycle who instructs by demonstration, as well as by encouraging participation in actual performance.

Song and instruments alike, however, vary little in the way

they are rendered. Lacking in aural contrasts, it is evident that music follows closely the bland, often barely undulating topography of the land itself, particularly about the plains country of the inland. The earth sounds generated by clapsticks (undergowth crackling underfoot, brush fires moving through the grassland) blend easily with the more gutteral tones of the didgeridoo. The sound of the didgeridoo is unique among traditional instruments. Its mournful tones, deeply reverberative, appear to emanate from far below the earth itself, as if the Rainbow Serpent were ascending to the surface. In turn, the didgeridoo brings to aboriginal music the symbolism of caves, rock chasms filled with wind, animals ruminating in burrows, the unheard noise that ants make in their nests if that sound were magnified sufficiently for the human ear to recognize. The instrument is truly chthonian, drawing its tones from a source that is but an echo of the origin of all music.

It is interesting to note that among the Pintupi people of Central Australia the melody of a song is known as the 'scent' (*mayu*) or 'taste' (*ngurru*). Both these words suggest a non-abstract notion of music, as if it possessed a physical presence of its own. This idea of a song possessing a body of its own is further enhanced by the fact that, like body decorations, each section of a song-cycle belongs to a person; while the entire song-cycle belongs to a clan or tribal grouping. Thus, in order for a song-cycle to achieve complete 'identity' it must be rendered by the entire group, or be sung in response to different sacred spots within the country of the owner(s). The song is created out of the land itself, and therefore cannot be forgotten. If a section of the song is not rendered for some reason, this is known as *püititjunanyi*, or 'making a hole' in the song — a further suggestion of the song as something 'made', not conceived.

It is clear that the Aboriginal nomad, because of his desire to move about his country (whether for nourishment or ritual purposes), has chosen a minimalist life-style. His cherished beliefs, the methods and symbols by which he gives these expression — all of them he carries about with him, not as artifacts but as ideas. In this sense, the Aboriginal nomad is the complete intellectual. He has no need to 'write down' in any permanent fashion the substance of his thought, since the act of rendering it permanent only diminishes intellectual contact with the material that delineates his metaphysical and cultural identity. This is one reason why so much material is considered to be secret-sacred — that is, it can only be encountered by fellow initiates who have experienced the deeper meaning, and understand the full metaphor of the land they traverse as nomads. For the Aborigine is acutely conscious of how fragile his inner life is. He knows that the esoteric truths that form the bedrock of any knowledge of the Dreaming, if they were to become known to a wider circle of non-initiates, would soon degenerate into mere folktales and popular lore. There is room for these in his world too, of course, but not at the expense of sacred law. Sacred law represents the core of his spiritual and intellectual being; without it, there would be no reason for him to embark upon his ritual wanderings throught time and space.

Everything in an Aborigine's country becomes a manifestation of the rapport that exists between himself and the realm of Dreaming. When he dances a *wantji wantji* or 'travel-dance', he is immediately transported into a state where all earth has the power to converse with him. When he sings a *tulku* he finds himself entering a condition where certain mystic information is imparted to him by his environment. As the Tjapangata clan were able to sing after two of their members had completed a Dream journey to a distant place, 'The two men saw an eaglehawk circling in the sky; it spoke to them.' These clan members were in turn invoking the mystery associated with a long myth — a myth that occupies space as well as different levels of metaphysical truth. In the process the eaglehawk — indeed the whole of earth — has become an avatar, an angel.

The idea of the earth as a manifestation of the Angel is a

very ancient concept. Certain Zoriastrian and Mazdain texts speak of celebrating a liturgy 'in honour of the Earth which is an Angel[9]. More recently, Gustav Fechner described an experience of a similar insight: 'I was walking in the open air on a beautiful spring morning. The wheat was growing green, the birds were singing, the dew was sparkling; the smoke rising; a transfiguring light lay over everything; this was only a tiny fragment of Earth . . . and yet the idea seemed to me not only so beautiful, but also true and so obvious that she was an Angel — an Angel so sumptuous, so fresh, like a flower and at the same time so firm and so composed, who was *moving through the sky* (our italics) . . .. that I asked myself how it was possible that men should have blinded themselves to the point of seeing the Earth as nothing but a dried-up mass and to the point where they go looking for Angels above them, or somewhere in the emptiness of Sky, and find them nowhere.'[10] He adds with melancholy that nowadays an experience like this would be dismissed as imaginary, in spite of our Tjapangata clan members having admitted to 'speaking' with the Angel in the guise of an eaglehawk.

Corbin himself suggests a new line of of study which he describes as *psychological geography*. Its intention, he believes, is to discover psychological factors that come into play in the conformation given to landscape. Implicit in any research of this kind would be that the essential functions of the soul, the *psyche*, include a nature, a *physis*. Conversely, each physical structure reveals the mode of *psycho-spiritual* activity that brings it into operation. Where psychological geography pertains to the Aboriginal perception of landscape as an extension to his spiritual life is in the 'categories of sacredness' that not only possess his soul, but also can be recognized in the landscape with which he surrounds himself. The geological shapes and habitat of this region in turn become the projected vision of an ideal iconography for him. He sees the earth about him as a model of the vision he has of the paradisal landscape — in other words, the realm of Dreaming. By mentally reconstructing the Dreaming in the form of sacred places and their associated mythology, he is able to keep company with the Angel, with Spirit-beings and his ancestors, with the avatars in the form of eaglehawks that look down at him while on the wing.[11]

Such a line of inquiry is in keeping with the inner landscape that the Aborigine retains as a nomad. Unlike the sederunt who projects his spiritual condition onto the world that he creates for himself, the Aborigine is content to *imagine* his spirituality by way of a variety of mnemonic and ritualistic devices. His body bears the sacred ideograms; his music and song recollect his mythic origins; his country represents the glorious forms of his inner world. These form a perfect hierophany which together make up the profound spiritual reality of the Aboriginal nomad. Such a view is reiterated by Bill Neidjie when he says, 'This story is important. It won't change, it is law. It is like this earth, it won't move. Ground and rock . . . he can't move. Cave . . . he never move. No-one can shift that cave, because it *dream* [our italics]. It story, it law. This law . . . this country . . . this people . . . no matter what people . . . red, yellow, black or white . . . the blood is the same. Lingo little bit different, but no matter. Country . . . you in other place, but same feeling. Blood, bone, all the same. This story, this is true story.'

This interrelationship between man and earth, between the need to wander through space in search of spiritual fulfillment and the desire to give cultural form to this pilgrimage, is at the very heart of the Aboriginal religious perspective. All but divested of clothing, surrounding himself as he does with so few possessions and at the mercy of a harsh climate, the Aborigine nevertheless has always been capable of defending himself against psychic terrors and the trauma of extreme isolation. He has done this by resorting to a rich imaginal life in the face of what must be considered a landscape of awesome loneliness. Because of the inherant *trust* that he has always displayed towards his environment, the Aboriginal nomad has never found the need to break the compact that he holds with

102

nature. As a result he has been able to engage in a dialogue with his country that takes for its syntax the untrammelled space in which he moves.

Notes

1. *The World of the Juki*, Douglas Halebi. Studies in Comparative Religion, 1983.

2. *Kakadu Man*, Big Bill Neidjie. Resource Managers' Darwin. 1987.

3. Genesis 3: 10: 'And he said, I heard thy voice in the garden, and I was afraid, because I was naked; and I hid myself.'

4. *The Decorated Body*, Robert Brain. 1979.

5. Ibid.

6. Ibid

7. Ibid.

8. *Songs of the Pintupi*, Richard M. Moyle. 1979.

9. *Spiritual Body and Celestial Earth*, pp 3, Henry Corbin. Bollingen Books.

10. Quoted by Corbin in his notes, pp 271.

11. Ibid. pp 30-31.

CHAPTER 7
The World of Totems

According to Aboriginal belief, mankind appears on earth as a reincarnation of a primordial being from the Dreaming. He comes into existence as the manifestation of a more rudimentary form of life to which he nevertheless owes his allegiance while he lives on earth. Man is, in a sense, incomplete, living the life of a shade in the stygean realm of the Dreaming. Until he is transformed by the self-existent Sky Hero known as Numbakulla (Arunta language) into a true man, he is condemned to living the life of an *Inapertwa*, possessing neither limbs nor senses, unable to eat, yet inextricably contained in an amorphous human sphere in which the limbs and body are only vaguely discernable. This condition of shapelessness, when a man is little more than a small red pebble, is known by the Arunta as *Kuruna*, a term that suggests man's pre-existent Form, his archítype.[1]

His spirit, however, does not necessarily manifest itself as some pre-existent ideal of beauty; but rather takes for its form the manifestation of an intermediate stage in life. Thus a man represents the transformation of a simpler, less complex condition of existence into one of completeness. He derives his origin from nature, whether it be animal, plant, material object, water, fire, wind, cloud or stars. His *origin*, so to speak, is as infinitely diverse as the manifestations of nature on earth. Indeed the Aborigine sees himself as the apotheosis of nature, a living pre-figurement of an ancestor now inhabiting the Dreaming.

This is why Aborigines identify with totems; for a totem is an embodiment of each individual in his or her primordial state. That is, before the individual was born into the world. The totem, therefore, represents an Aborigine's pre-existent condition, his contact with the Dreaming. Without it he is unable to identify with his primordial state or metaphysical

105

persona, since he would have lost contact with the Dreaming altogether. The totem is a sacred link with the Dreaming, with a man's incarnation as a human being, with the Sky Heroes who created him. To sever this connection is to destroy a man's spirit and ultimately his desire to live. Indeed it is impossible for an Aborigine to 'lose' his totem, except by way of cultural disruption as in the case of many urban Aborigines unfortunate enough not to have been born within a totemic environment.

Possessing a totem, or having been conceived in a particular totemic environment, is a form of baptism. A man is 'born' into the witchetty grub or emu totem, for example, the moment his mother acknowledges conception within that totemic environment. Even if she happens to be of another totem herself, a woman must acknowledge where the spirit children, or *Kurunas*, chose to enter her body. From that moment on, the unborn child is an embryo of an ancestral being in the process of transformation from an *Inapertwa* — that is, an incomplete man — into a divine human being. For the revelation or divination of an Aborigine as someone intimately identified with his Dreaming ancestor is far more important than acknowledging the accident of biological parentage. Man is not *conceived* as such by other individuals, but by the willful act of the Sky Heroes. A man's conception is the result of a desire on the part of these ancestral beings to bring into being a more complete spiritual entity.

Once a man's divine origin is acknowledged by way of his totem, it is encumbent on him to revere his 'alter-ego' for the duration of his life. He 'is' a sea-eagle, or a dingo, fire or a crocodile even as he is a man. The two conditions of existence are interchangeable in that there is no logical hiatus between them. As one informant remarked, "Sea-eagle and me, we one body."[2] Clearly this man wanted us to recognize the mutuality that existed between himself and the giant raptor in view. His incarnation as a human being was contiguent with that of the bird in question. Another informant remarked, "Your Dreaming is there [ie. totem]. It is a big thing. You never let it go. All Dreamings [totems] come from there. Your spirit is there."[3] Here the informant is asking us to acknowledge the divine origin of his persona in that realm of otherness known as the Dreaming.

As a result of this association with his totem, an Aborigine is required to enhance his relationship with his totem by way of certain ritual or taboo acts. If his totem happens to be a potential foodstuff, for example, he will only eat of it sparingly, if at all. And then he will not eat the best parts, only the fat. This is because he is, as it were, 'eating himself', an act of self-absorption that is ritually — and more probably psychologically — profoundly distasteful to him.

The relationship, then, between an Aborigine and his totem is one of consumate identification. He or she enters into a relationship that is not only life-long, but life-giving. Being born into, or of a totem predisposes a person to ritual acceptance of what is, after all, his unique identity on this earth. Knowing that his totem has been determined by his Dreaming ancestors, an Aborigine cannot escape, no does he wish to, the totemic environment into which he is born. Indeed the spiritual terrain of his existence, his 'country' as it is often known as, is largely determined by his place of conception — that is, where the *kuruna* entered his mother's body. Thus he will always regard the land of his totem as the very bedrock of his being; and, like an icon, his totem hovers before his consciousness, an object of veneration that is in no way diminished by its commonality with others. In fact, in most cases, when a man finds that he shares a totem with another, then these men automatically become brothers. In that sense a totem becomes 'a sign of unity between things or persons *unified by something else.*'[4]

It is at this point that we begin to perceive a metaphysical dimension that is no longer merely abstract. Identifying with a totem invokes a range of emotions that are both historical and mystical. They are historical in the sense that they evoke memories of conception; they are mystical in the sense that they trigger a deeper urge towards unity by way of the totem itself. The totem is a key by which the door to the Dreaming is unlocked. Men may talk about the Dreaming, they may enact rituals that serve to confirm its existence as the 'otherworld'; but it is only by way of the totem that a man can actually experience his oneness with the Dreaming condition itself.

This relationship between a man and his totem, or a man and his Dreaming ancestor, however, is not confined to a spiritual concept only. It does have a physical counterpart which in itself embodies the numen. According to myth, at the time of the World Creation the Sky Heroes wandered together in totemic companies across the land, giving form to it as they went. These spirit-beings carried with them a bundle of sacred stones which were associated with the *Kuruna*, or the spirit-part of the individual, and were known by the Arunta as *Churinga*. These *Churinga* were, in a sense, a physical remnant of the Sky Heroes' immortal souls, and as such became sacred objects that must be protected and preserved.

In the course of their world-creating activities the Sky Heroes camped in various places which in turn became totem centres, or *Knanikilla*. Often the Sky Hero might have disappeared into the ground or have died here, thus making these spots important ritual sites for later generations of Aborigines. Such sacred places were known only to the old men of the tribe, since it was here that the *Churinga* of the various Sky Heroes remained as evidence of their passing at the time of the Dreaming. These *Churinga* were then stored in sacred storehouses known as *Pertalchera*, which usually took the form of caves, fissures in rock or hollowed out trees. Here the spirit-individuals or *Kuruna* associated with each *Churinga* was housed as a living reminder of the Sky Heroes' timeless presence. Like the relics of saints, *Churinga* are an object of veneration, pilgrimage and the basis of important rites.

Thus there are important *Churinga* associated with the Sky Heroes which were made by 'divine hand', not by man. These carved stones have been in the totem-centres since the beginning of time and are inevitably filled with *djang*, or numenous power. They can only be handled by Elders of the particular totemic group, and are never revealed to the women or non-initiates. It is as if these *Churinga* represented a direct spiritual link with the Dreaming. By handling them, by rubbing a finger over them during the course of a song-cycle or ceremony, a man is capable of invoking the spirit of the Sky Hero with such intensity that his 'real' presence is felt by all those nearby.

This is not to say that a man does not have a *Churinga* of his own. In many parts of Australia the custom prevails that the paternal grandfather of the the newly born child must go into the bush in the region of the totem-centre belonging to that child's totem and make a wooden *Churinga* out of wood found on a tree nearby. The *Churinga* is then ornamented with designs belonging to the child's totem. However, such a *Churinga* is not considered to embody the *Kuruna* of the Sky Hero, but merely serves as a reminder to the child of the existence of the original stone *Churinga* housed at the totem-centre. His personal *Churinga* is but an 'echo' or the original *Churinga*, said to have been fashioned by the Sky Hero. The *Churinga* does, however, act as a direct link with the Dreaming, and is invariably placed in the youth's hands after circumcision. Touching the *Churinga* for the first time brings him in contact with the numenous power of the Dreaming. He is now 'joined' by way of his *Churinga* (representing his totem) to the original moment of creation. At once he partakes of the continuity and order associated with the Dreaming to the point where he has now begun to transcend his social persona in the interest of acknowledging his divine entity. The *Churinga* becomes, in the words of Plotinus, a 'manifestation of knowledge and wisdom as a distinct image, an object in itself, an immediate unity'.[5]

In the course of time a personal *Churinga* becomes so bound up with an individual that it finally acquires a certain *djang* of its own. This *djang*, however, is normally associated with the individual owner, particularly after death, rather than with the Sky Hero or totem that it represents. A personal *Churinga* can thereby endow its owner, or even someone who subsequently possesses it, with the qualities and attributes of its original owner. Thus a personal *Churinga* in time may grow to acquire something of the archetypal *djang* associated with the Sky Hero himself, although it still retains its personal dimension in keeping with the individual who once owned it.

Belonging to a particular totem is a a form of spiritual heraldry for the Aborigine. He cannot escape the implications of belonging to a totemic environment in terms of its demands upon him. A totem bestows upon a man his identity, not only in a personal sense but in a transcendent sense. When the first *Churinga* were made by the Sky Hero, Numbakulla, he was at pains to make these perfect in conformity with the archetypes. By splitting these original *Churinga* in two, however, it was possible to obtain pairs of *Churinga* that were embued with the spirits of both male and female. In the process a state of duality was imposed upon the world which could only be eliminated, symbolically, by tying together each pair of one *Churinga*. Thus the cleavage between the Dreaming and the world of manifestation could be restored in a way that preserved the memory, at least, of what the original pristine condition of the world had once been.

In keeping with the sacred nature of the *Churinga* and its esoteric significance, the object bears a secret name, known as an *Aritna Churinga*, that has been bestowed upon it by the Sky Hero, Numbakulla. As these original *Churinga* gave birth to numerous *Kurunas*, or spirits, which in turn gave rise to men and women, these secret names were then bestowed upon those people of the respective totems. Hence a man or a women bears a spiritual name beside that of his or her 'family' name. The *Aritna Churinga* thereby correctly identifies the person for what he or she truly is: a spiritual being who is enmeshed in the timeless net of the Dreaming that has been thrown over the mortal husk by the Sky Heroes.

It is clear from the foregoing that the totem and its link with those *Churinga* emanating from the Dreaming are a vital part of Aboriginal belief. By way of the totem an Aborigine is capable of discerning his connection with the so-called 'First People' of the Dreaming. The presence, too, of sanctified objects held in trust in the landscape are further proof of spiritual descent from the Dreaming. Aborigines desire knowledge and contact with their spiritual parents. They long to unveil certain numenosities applicable to their origins, even if it does require the active and time-honoured support of symbolism to aid this process. In Plotinus' words, 'All teems with symbol; the wise man is the man who in any one thing can read another'.[6] In this case, the *Churinga* becomes the active symbol, the bearer of numen.

Thus we are made aware of the Aborigine's continuing desire to remain in touch with the Dreaming. It is a fact that Aboriginal culture is profoundly theocratic and rarely strays into secular activity, except at the very basic, practical level. It is this theocentricity, however, that most confronts the modern Western mind because of its intense, praise-oriented function. The modern mind finds it difficult to understand a culture that is primarily directed towards a metaphysical pole at the expense of so-called material wellbeing. The illusion that the Western mind is burdened with in this context is that theocratic concerns are basically antipathetic to so-called 'ordinary' human experience. The modern mind cannot comprehend how much joy and universal wellbeing is unleashed upon an environment in the very act of celebrating the relationship between Aboriginal man and the Dreaming. In the words of the Koran, 'The seven heavens and the earth and all that is therein praise Him, and there is not a thing that does not hymn His praise.'[7]

Thus the totem and its associated *Churinga* are powerful reminders of the ever-present numenosity of the Dreaming. Indeed the land itself is one vast *Churinga* that does 'hymn His praise' in the eyes of Aborigines. Such a concept goes to the very root of the Aborigine's reverence for land. Popular clichés such as 'the earth she my mother' merely reinforce what every Aborigine knows in his heart to be true: that the world below reflects an ideal condition above. But where the Aboriginal viewpoint differs from many other traditional peoples is that the Dreaming is a timeless reality that can be approached, indeed entered, on this earth. Myth and ritual are only adjuncts to this process. The real entry-point is by way of a transformation of the individual — a transformation that can only be brought about when a person attains to a state of hieratical dignity.

In this sense the *Churinga*, and the totem that it represents, prefigures a paradisal landscape, what the Mazdeans called the 'landscape of *Xvarnah*'. This is a landscape in which everything is transfigured by that light of glory the soul projects onto it. As a nomadic people the Aborigines project most of their inner beliefs onto their tribal landscape, since they are not able to construct edifices to reflect their metaphysical ideals. The earth becomes the manifestation of a vision, of a visionary geography,[8] in which the soul can meet and converse with its maker by way of symbolic and ritual expression. This in turn means that the Aboriginal hierophant must mentally re-constitute the Dreaming here on earth if he wishes to attain to a level of consciousness that allows him access to the Dreaming condition. This is one reason why Aboriginal earth painting, particularly in Central Australia, bears so little similarity to the actual material landscape of the tribe. For the painter, when he is painting 'his' country, or his Dreaming, is not painting a physical landscape at all; he is painting a visionary landscape that not only conforms to his *Churinga* or totem, but to the perception that has been handed down to him of the Dreaming landscape of his totem by his forebears. As one commentator puts it, 'the pilgrims of the spirit contemplate this world and in it find every object of their desire.'[9] The Aborigine is therefore able to project a visionary landscape that satisfies both his yearning towards identification with the Sky Heroes and his Dreaming ancestors.

This is not to say that Aborigines recognize the Sky Heroes as the divine emanation of godhead. But clearly the Sky Heroes have performed, in their eyes, an avataric function when they descended to earth and 'created' the land. It is evident that Aborigines are beholden to the Sky Heroes as true creator-beings, even if godlike attributes are withheld. The Sky Heroes are simply spirit-beings whose withdrawal into the Dreaming at a point outside time is accepted as being a para-normal event. Such a withdrawal, however, does not preclude acknowledging these spirit-beings as objects of veneration. Indeed their place in the hierarchy of creation makes it mandatory that they are venerated.

Clearly an Aborigine is in the presence of an important revelation about his relationship with the Dreaming, and about his spiritual destiny in the world when he encounters his totem in the form of its *Churinga*. In an orally based culture such as theirs, it is evident that the *Churinga* acts as a 'text' which can be consulted at any given time. By touching the *Churinga* during ceremonies, by allowing it to invoke the Dreaming songs associated with a man's totem, the *Churinga* acts as a meditational aid not unlike the rosary. Since Aborigines, like so many other traditional peoples, are deeply bonded to physical objects as a method of expressing their own spiritual state, the *Churinga* must be regarded as a significant cultural object. Like the Tooth of Mohammed or a Piece of the True Cross, the *Churinga* is a relic in the true sense, since it is imbued with a meta-history that transcends all other personal or mythic data.

Nor is this relationship static. The assumption that the *Churinga* (and therefore a man's totem) is a fetish object, incapable of reflecting any change in the individual, presumes that an Aborigine is incapable himself of undergoing spiritual growth. This is the kind of criticism that all traditional peoples have long had to put up with, simply because their religious belief defies logical analysis. Aboriginal religion in particular is chthonic in essence, and therefore stems from a different intellective source than conventional universal religions. But this does not mean it is not in possession of the 'metaphysical gift' so jealously guarded by more established theologies. From 'where' or 'how' men derive their spiritual sustenance is less important than the intensity of veneration bestowed upon that source. In this sense the Aborigines are proud exemplars of an ancient race who have allowed religion, and religious belief, to saturate their lives.

, Indeed few other cultures in the history of mankind have so successfully integrated their religious belief with the normal activities of their lives as these people. The totem and its *Churinga* are an intimate part of this process. It is is as if the *Churinga* acts as a Bridge of Chinvat over which the soul of Aboriginal man journeys into the realm of the Dreaming. Living in accordance with his totem, a man is then able to cross this bridge and encounter his Dreaming ancestor, his 'celestial Idea', so to speak. Resisting his totem is to betray what he stands for, his honour, indeed his essential nature. In many ways this accounts for the cultural collapse of the Aboriginal people in the wake of European dominance during the past two hundred years. By divorcing Aborigines from their land, these people in consequence have been separated from their totems. In doing so the bridge linking them with their 'celesial Idea', their Dreaming, has been destroyed. It is any wonder, then, that alcoholism and cultural disorientation have ensued.

The totem, therefore, is the man. He stands by his elected ancestor, his Dreaming guide. Conception grants him a unique identity, a spirit identity which is not only of him, but of the Dreaming. This spirit or *Kuruna* takes the form of a little bird called a *Chichurkna* whose whistling is often heard when there has been a death in camp. At once this little bird flies away to the totem site of the dead man where it joins up with its double, the *Arumburinga*, in order that they might both protect the man's body from attacks by mischievous spirits. It is at this point that we recognize the 'pairing' once more of the dual spirits that have been watching over the man in life. The

Chichurkna of the man unites with the *Arumburinga* of the man's *Churinga*, thus giving rise once more to a totemic wholeness in the Dreaming.[10]

Birth, for Aborigines, is a supernatural event. Being born into a totemic environment releases a man from the chains of mortality. Though his body dies, his spirit always remains in its totemic environment. His world-view, the Dreaming, magnifies its presence in his life by way of the totem. Therefore he is able to move about the earth, fearing only a dissolution brought on by non-belief or separation from the land of his totem. The totem is his bond with the infinite. Aboriginal man has created for himself a supreme theophany through his deep reverence for the Dreaming. The essential community between visible and invisible things is re-affirmed by way of the totem and its *Churinga*. Thus 'suns and moons can be seen in an earthly state and in the heavens all the plants, stones, animals in a heavenly state, living spiritually'.[11] It is this sentiment that most exemplifies the effect of a totem on a man's spiritual life. Through it he can visualize, in his intellect, the full theophanic glory of the Dreaming.

Notes

1. *Coming into Being among Australian Aborigines*. Ashley Montagu, Routledge & Kegan Paul.

2. Author's field notes.

3. *White Man Got No Dreaming*. W.E.H. Stanner. A.N.U. Press.

4. Ibid. pp129.

5. *The Enneads*. V 8.6. Plotinus, Faber & Faber.

6. Ibid. II 3.7.

7. *The Koran*. The Pilgrimage Sura (XVII:45), Oxford World Classics.

8. See *Spiritual Body and Celestial Earth* by Henry Corbin (Bollingen Series) for a detailed analysis of Visionary Geography.

9. *Oeuvres philosopheiques et mystiques de Sohrawardi*. Suhrawardi

10. A comparison could be made with the ancient Egyptians' concept of *Ba* and *Ka*. A man's *Ka* is invariably portrayed as a tiny bird which departs the body at death. It is said that when a man is *master of his Ka*, and *goes with his Ka*,

then he is alive. Since death is the separation of the subtle from the corporeal, the *Ka* must then fly to its *Ba* in the same way as the *Chichurkna* must fly to its *Arumburinga*. The papyrus texts say that the *Ba must recover its Ka* for any rebirth or resurrection is to take place. This is in keeping with the Aboriginal perception of the Spirit's return to the the Dreaming, to be re-united — and by implication — reborn in the ancestral totem.

11. *Treatise on the Hieratic Art of the Greeks*. Proclus.

CHAPTER 8
Solitude and Community

Paulinous of Nola, writing to his pagan friend Ausonius early in the fifth century, spoke of the solitary state in a way that has conditioned how we think of solitude and the hermit ever since:

> Not that they be beggared in mind, or brutes,
> Because they have chosen to live in lonely places:
> Their eyes are turned to the high stars,
> The very stillness of truth.[1]

It is essentially a self-centred concept of the man who withdraws from society in order to pursue a spiritual life in the uncluttered precinct of the desert or the forest. By the early fifth century the Christian anchorite movement of Egypt and Palestine had been in existence for well over one hundred years, and its social effects had jolted both peasant and patrician alike throughout the Roman world. Since then Western monasticism, at least as we know it in Europe and in Russia, has canonized solitary behaviour by way of fasts, silences and ritualized forms of penitence. It is not for nothing that St Isaac of Syria exhorted wayward monks to choose loneliness and exile if they wish to progress in a life of virtue.[2]

But for the Australian Aborigine the idea of quitting the tribal community in order to seek out solitude is entirely alien to his thinking. It is not that he is unaware of the psychological effects of aloneness; but that he sees his act of solitude in terms of its social effect. To understand his behaviour one must first understand the complex metaphysical relationship an Aborigine has with the landscape, and how his Dreaming country conditions all his actions. For, in the sense that Paulinous of Nola meant it, or St Jerome when he wrote of St Anthony, an Aborigine cannot be alone in a desert place,

117

except when he leaves his tribal country. Wherever he might happen to be in terms of tribal nomadic patterns, he will always find himself in close proximity to his ancestors, to his Dreaming cult-heroes (Sky Heroes) and to his totemic birthplace. An Aborigine, even when he is physically alone, lives in, and is sustained by, a metaphysical community.

The Aborigine, unlike his modern counterpart, relies on a small range of utensils and weapons to sustain himself. Living in the bush, he has been able to survive a minimalist lifestyle for upwards of 50,000 years. Post Ice-age inundation may have periodically limited the arrival of new migrants to Australia from Asia, and therefore new technological advances from which he might draw benefit. Nevertheless, it is doubtful whether he might have wished for any further improvements to his lifestyle, given that he had worked out a successful *modus vivendi* in keeping with his environment. His so-called 'backwardness' was not as a result of any intellectual incapacity as might have been suggested by nineteenth-century ethnologists, but as a result of his priorities: he had long ago decided that his spiritual life was more important to him than his physical life.

So the ascetic principle does not exist for him as a separate reality. He does not need to withdraw from the tribal community in order to work out his salvation. This is taken care of in the context of tribal belief, custom and law. He is beholden to these before he is beholden to himself. The law of the community takes precedence over, and largely subsumes, any individual volition of his own. The Aborigine sees himself as a member of a tribe first before he sees himself as an individual. This is not to say that his social identity eliminates all sense of individual persona — far from it. Aborigines are most singular in their presence, conscious of their totemic and matrilineal identity, which makes each person unique in terms of his or her community relationships.

In an earlier chapter I have written at length about the Aborigine's relationship with the earth. Like all traditional peoples, he is deeply bonded to his tribal country by a set of beliefs and rituals. These take the form of his totemic identity, the songs and dances associated with his totem, the esoteric lore pertaining to his Dreaming place (where he was conceived by way of his spirit's 'entry' into his mother's body, not as a result of any physical liaison between his parents), and the Sky Hero activity linked to the creation of the world at the time of the Dreaming. For it is the timeless moment of the Dreaming, when the world 'was new', as one tribal elder so eloquently described it to me, that prefigures all existence. This is no paradisial state, nor is it a primordial condition; but a concept that embraces continued ancestral existence *post mortem*, as well as the moment when the world first became manifest. Various Sky Heroes are identified with this creation process, the most important being the Rainbow Serpent. His iconic presence is seen on cave walls throughout Australia, and features prominently in myth, story and song. Many water-holes, too, are sacred to his name. The spring of Mutitdjilda, for instance, lying at the foot of Uluru (Ayers Rock), is sacred to Wanambi, the Rainbow Serpent.

Since the Sky Heroes created the world (i.e. the hills, the watercourses, the valleys, individual stones and unusual landmarks), tribal territory becomes a complex grid of mythic expression. An Aborigine can never escape the hiero-history of his people, except in a wilful act of amnesia. Therefore he is constantly in contact with a metaphysical perspective which conditions his way of thinking and acting. Indeed Aboriginal activity is often fraught with restrictions in the form of taboos, as tribal law figures large in his scheme of things. In spite of the seeming endlessness of space, and the idea of an un-peopled landscape which the early white settlers considered the continent to represent, an Aborigine is conscious that wherever he walks he confronts the remnants of mythic drama and its concomitant prohibitions. A man does not walk free into a desert landscape as the ancient Christian anchorites might have seen themselves doing; instead he is forever living within mythic territory created by ancestral heroes.

The concept of solitude as it is conventionally understood does not exist for the Aborigine. His dialogue is not with himself or with his Maker, but with the realm of hieratic activity — a realm governed by supra-mundane events. There is no identification between himself and a monotheistic god. This is not to say that he has no concept of the numinous presence, or that the hiero-figure is not a part of his world. Rather, he does not recognize a personal relationship between himself and the otherness of the Sky Hero. The Sky Hero simply exists, or existed at the time of the Dreaming. The divine entity lives another life, a supernatural life, a life governed by celestial laws not pertaining to the human order. The Aborigine acknowledges two levels of reality which do not intersect, except during ritual activity when the channels of communication are deliberately opened. This means that man lives one sort of life, a mortal life, while the Sky Hero lives another sort of life, a celestial life.

A state of solitude can only exist for an Aborigine when the world of the Sky Hero — that is, the world of the Dreaming — is denied him. Even when a young warrior is required to undergo tribal initiation and quit the tribe, sometimes for many months, his temporary exile does not mean that he is living beyond the frontier of culture. For he carries with him knowledge, limited perhaps (since he has not been fully initiated, and so certain esoteric information has been withheld), but nevertheless contiguent to the country over which he wanders. He is not set loose upon an alien landscape intellectually or spiritually blindfolded. He 'knows where he is going' since he is familiar with the mythic symbols at his disposal. This means that while he might be alone in the physical sense, he is not acting out a solitary existence in the way an anchorite might be attempting to do in his cave in the desert. The anchorite deliberately attempts to *deprive* himself of the significance of his physical reality, whereas the Aborigine sets out to consort with his.

Solitude, at least as we understand it, presupposes a rejection of all that we might consider as the 'illusion of sensibility'. The anchorite or the solitary set out to remove themselves from the web of ordinary reality in order to pursue a life of spiritual gnosis. In the process they often find themselves engaging in what Lorenzo Scupoli termed 'unseen warfare' with demons and negative psychic phenomena. These in turn lead to a further desire to practise increasing austerities in the hope of purging the soul of its impurities. The physical appetites are finally pacified to the point where both mind and spirit are able to partake of a state of bliss. It is the ultimate objective for all ascetics, whether they are Christian, Buddhist, Hindu or Moslem. The solitary life is intimately associated with the desire to transcend contingent reality in the expectation of experiencing another order of reality altogether. It is the basis of all modern spiritual practice.

But for the Aborigine the idea of depriving himself of aspects of this life in order to embrace a particular spiritual condition pertaining to another life does not figure largely in his scheme of things. This is not to say that he does not understand the benefits of ascetic activity: he does. Most initiatory ritual involves physical deprivation of some sort. Body scarification, tooth-knocking, circumcision, subincision (where the penis is split in two), such practices are designed to test a postulant so that he is able to resist pain. Physical pain is regarded as an important adjunct to the business of deepening one's awareness of manhood. Indeed an Aborigine often voluntarily subjects himself to mutilation at different times of his life so as to prove to himself, and to his tribal elders, what level of interiority he has attained as a man of knowledge, a 'man of high degree'.[3]

Formalized ascetic practices are derived from community perceptions of how to attain to a more luminous spirituality. They are devised largely by cenobitic groups, which implies a community, or in urban environments. That they are practised in remote places (the monastery must be considered as a symbolic 'remote place') merely emphasises the importance of deprivation and pain as methods by which spiritual insight is evoked. These methods are common to all humanity, except in the case of the genuine atheist or agnostic, although he, too, will probably acknowledge their salutary effect, even if he denies their efficacy. To a certain extent the idea of 'passing over' into another condition determines how we feel about normal reality. In this sense the Aborigine is acutely aware of the need to pass over, or make contact with a supernal reality. Indeed this perception conditions much of his life. Ascetic practice that is derived from the concept of solitude, however, relies not upon seeking out 'lonely places' (although these abound), but in opening up the channels of communication between himself and the Sky Heroes.

Ritual is the instrument by which the Aborigine explores the otherworld, the Dreaming. He is the supreme liturgist, capable of devising ceremonies to embrace all aspects of Sky Hero activity, whether they be real or imagined. Ritual is the material delineation of the metaphysical and imaginal faculties.[4] By embodying the immaterial in an action (dance) or a musical construct (song), he gives physical credence to a range of numinous values and emotions.Equally, by linking ritual to various ascetic practices (circumcision, blood-mingling as a method of signifying divine brotherhood) on the occasion of major tribal ceremonies, such a nexus affirms the invisible presence of the Sky Heroes, and so denotes the consanguinity between man and spirit. Ascetic activity is therefore rarely detached from ritual in the Aboriginal context. Although the idea of *self*-flagellation is entirely alien to him, he does not want to attain to spiritual knowledge outside the tribal forum. He is brother to his kind, and his spiritual life is intimately associated with the collective spiritual life of his community.

Thus solitude takes on an entirely different meaning for the Aborigine. His landscape is an extended myth. He does not live 'off' the land, but 'in' a terranean relationship with the otherworld, the Dreaming. His association with birds and animals also partakes of confraternity not separateness. These are a part of his totemic life, which means that their existence is an echo of his own. So that a man can never be alone in a landscape when he knows that he is not only living within proximity of myth (the Sky Hero), but within physical proximity of his totem. He is enclosed within an envelope made up of hiero-history and its natural counterpart, the totem. Physical solitude can only be realized when these conditions are absent.

If a landscape becomes 'dead' as a bearer of hiero-history, or when the animals have departed (a form of physical 'deadness') because ritual life has abated, then a tribal territory is in danger of becoming a metaphysical desert. A man walking out on such a landscape, not knowing or no longer able to recall the Dreaming events associated with it, will find himself entering a state of existential solitude, the solitude brought on by metaphysical *angst*. On my travels I have often met Aborigines who regretfully relate to me how the stories belonging to a particular piece of country have been 'forgotten', or that its custodian ('key-man') has died without passing on the stories related to its Dreaming existence. Once this has happened, it is unlikely that the land will again be a part of the community of men. Often it becomes 'rubbish country', a term Aborigines use to denote country devoid of its hiero-history. It has become, literally, a mythical and metaphysical desert.

As an example of how the intimacy between an Aborigine and his land can work, and how an act of solitude inevitably partakes of a numinous experience, I would like to relate a story told to one observer by the celebrated dancer, Leotardi, from Milingimbi in Arnhemland, Northern Territory. Explaining how he created his songs and dances, Leotardi said:

123

'The spirits give them to me. Sometimes when I am out hunting I come to a certain place. Something in that place tells me to keep quiet. By and by I see the spirits come out and start singing and dancing. They are painted up, and they are beating the song-sticks together. I keep quiet. I catch that song. I catch that dance. I catch that painting. I come back to the camp and give this song, this dance, this painting to my people.'[5]

Here we have a typical explanation of the way a man draws upon his country in order to create forms of expression that denote his relationship with that piece of country. His act of solitude immediately places him in contact with metaphysical information which in turn he hands on to his community. At no time does he see himself possessing it for himself alone; the spirits are offering him material which is the property of all men, namely his tribal brothers. What underlies Leotardi's encounter with his country, however, is a relationship with otherness. I hesitate to use the word 'mystical' as its connotation today implies a fervour, an abandon, which Aborigines do not acknowledge in their spiritual practice.

Nevertheless Leotardi does acknowledge seeing the spirits. They reveal themselves to him. They have a physical, an imaginal presence. More importantly, perhaps, he recognizes that *something in the land tells him to keep quiet*. Clearly he has entered into a numinous dialogue with the spirit of the land, a dialogue which we might term as the basis for prayer. I think this is important to understand: that the Aborigine, whereas he may not have a personal relationship with deity, does have a personal relationship with the earth as a numinous entity. Insofar as the earth is capable of silencing him, he sees himself as participating in spiritual fraternity with his country. The country has control over him. It acts as his spiritual guide, his comforter.

True exile for an Aborigine could only involve the abandonment of his birthright — that is, his Dreaming. Not only would such an event involve his spiritual death, but in many cases his physical death might ensue also. Robinson relates a story told to him by a New South Wales Aborigine of a man who sold a mountain to the mayor of a local town to be used as a quarry. The mayor offered the tribal owner a few sovereigns and a bottle of rum as payment. Meanwhile the first charge of gelignite set under the mountain unleashed a stream of black water which took many weeks to dry up.In that time the tribal owner of the mountains fell sick and died. His Dreaming had been so damaged by the explosion that the man himself was mortally wounded. As Robinson's informant later remarked, the man had sold his birthright, his Dreaming.[6]

As mentioned earlier, landscape is imbued with *djang*, a numinous power which denotes the spiritual vitality of the earth. Aborigines accept that most landscapes actually live, and therefore cannot be classified as wilderness. Unlike the anchorite who regards his cave as the embodiment of a material vacuity, the Aborigine sees his landscape as a spiritual panorama populated by spirits. He calls this concentration of telluric energy *djang* or *kurunba*, depending on which tribe he belongs to. He therefore embraces his country as his mother, not as inchoate material there to be exploited for material purposes. What happened to the owner of the mountain when the gelignite exploded was the recognition that the *djang* of the place had been destroyed.He had allowed its spiritual vitality to be decimated. From then on this country would have been classified as 'rubbish country', and so condemned to a more or less vitiated existence outside the community of men. The suggestion is obvious: that men alone do not make up a community; it requires the participation of the land to augment the principles of good citizenship, what the ancients knew as *civitas*.

To talk of the desire for solitude as an existential condition similar to the idea of contentment or wellbeing in terms of Aboriginal spirituality is to denigrate the overall metaphysical environment they inhabit. Aborigines do not seek solitude in the way that other spirituals might. Nor do they regard landscape as a place set apart where one can isolate oneself from the community. Of course they acknowledge the reality of sacred places, many of which may be found in remote regions. But their remoteness is incidental to their spiritual significance as active participants in the hieratic pageant known as the Dreaming. As Bill Neidjie, the Bunidji tribesman, remarked: 'Earth . . . like your father or brother or mother, because you born from earth. You got to come back to earth. When you're dead . . . you'll come back to earth. Maybe little bit while yet . . . then you'll come back to earth. That's your bone, your blood. It's in this earth, same as for tree.'[7]

Sentiments such as these poignantly express how an Aborigine feels about his environment. It is virtually impossible for him to deny his relationship with earth, with his Dreaming, with his totem. This triad conditions his intellectual and emotional outlook. It also conditions his attitude towards his community. Although he does recognize the need to retire from the community on ceremonial occasions, the sense of solitude he engenders at this time is carefully orchestrated by way of myth and ritual. He therefore is never 'alone' as such, never finds himself afflicted by what the anchorites knew as 'acidie', or profound spiritual boredom.

So complete and overreaching is the Dreaming that an Aborigine would find it difficult to break free and become 'self-conscious' in the way we understand it, because his self cannot be detached from the web of relationships that he has with his mother, his father, his totemic kindred and the land which made him. He is both prisoner and freeman, at once a victim of metaphysical certitude and its exemplar. His personal identity is fashioned from abstract mythic material and the invisible workings of the earth. Therefore he is able to transcend many personal limitations (being a bad father, or a poor spear-thrower, for example) when he enters into the spirit of his other self, his totemic identity. It means that an Aborigine is capable of more than one life, his physical life. He is also capable of a profoundly imaginal life, a life in league with a sense of otherness.

The Aborigine is not an ancient individual, the remnant of some pre-historic race as many commentators have assumed in the past. Rather he is a man of culture, someone who never strays far from his origins. In this sense he is someone who is able to continually re-create his own celestial history without pinning down its beginning to some arbitrary point in time. The Dreaming occurred, and is still occurring. As a metaphysical condition it transcends time, casting its glow on all men, in all places at the one time, living or dead. Its spiritual dimension is so extensive that it is capable of displacing the material contingency of the here-and-now with a pervasive order. At this point the truly mysterious object of the Dreaming lies beyond all apprehension or comprehension, not only because knowledge has certain immovable limits, but because in it one comes upon something inherently 'wholly other' before which an Aborigine —as we all do — recoils in wonder. Thus the Dreaming embodies for the Aborigine all that is 'wholly other', all that informs him of his separate and unique identity.

Ultimately one must consider the Australian Aborigine as visible proof that the hiatus between man and nature is a comparatively recent phenomenon. Christians may wish to ascribe such a condition to the advent of the Fall; but an Aborigine believes otherwise. He is not afflicted with a deep concern for the immortality of his soul, provided of course that the mortuary ceremonies have been properly conducted. In this way his soul's safety is in the hands of fellow tribesmen, so he need not fear its demise. Its destination is the huge reservoir of Spirit[8] that lies, unplumbed, in the deeper recesses of the Dreaming. It is the here-and-now that interests him primarily, and he is at pains to adore the world of nature as its exemplar. He is content to live in this world and does not crave after another. For him solitude is a temporary condition which may or may not augment spiritual insight. Moreover the rituals are his true passport to chthonic gnosis, not prolonged isolation in some lonely landscape. His asceticism takes the form of an extreme gentility towards all things in nature, not self-inflicted penance.

Notes

1. Helen Waddell, *Mediaeval Latin Lyrics*, Penguin Classics, 1962.

2. Kadloubovsky and Palmer, *Early Fathers from the Philokalia*, Faber & Faber, 1969, p.239, para.190.

3. See A.P. Elkin, *Aboriginal Men of High Degree*, University of Queensland Press, 1977.

4. Corbin, Henry, 'Towards a Chart of the Imaginal', *Temenos* 1, 1981. Corbin identifies the imaginal world as the 'world of souls'. An imaginal form is a mediation between the intellectual and sensible worlds. In this sense, it is above the merely 'imaginative' which is often steeped in the sensible for its own sake. The imaginal form presupposes an encounter with Being and Knowledge, a theophany.

5. Roland Robinson, *The Man Who Sold His Dreaming*, Seal Books, 1965.

6. Ibid., pp.98-110.

7. Bill Neidjie, *Australia's Kakadu Man*, Resources Managers, Darwin, 1986.

8. The unmanifest principle is named, however. As Ngadaia or Baiami, a shadowy gnomon, the Spirit inhabits the Dreaming as the First Cause. Man does not enter into a relationship with it in any way. The Sky Heroes are the only medium of contact an Aborigine has with the Dreaming and, by implication, with Baiami. It is rare indeed that Baiami appears on earth; although I have encountered one sacred place said to be where he came to earth — a place known as Kumana Kira in the Pilbara region of Western Australia.

CHAPTER 9
Towards a New Dreaming

Throughout this book no attempt has been made to establish Aboriginal spirituality as a cohesive theology capable of being broken down into a tidy system of belief. Aboriginal religion has been poorly served by this approach in the past — an approach that for too long has been the mainspring of anthropological and social scientific inquiry. It is plainly evident that this confinement of the exploration of Aboriginal culture to the academic environment has lead to a malnourished vision of what Aboriginal spirituality is all about. In the process genuine intellectual intuition has been replaced by scholastic techniques masquerading as 'social science'.

This is not to say that there is no clearly defined 'creed' of belief among Aborigines. Far from it. The essential core of their spirituality is remarkably consistent throughout the country, in spite of the tribal isolation that has made communication so difficult in the past. In this respect one is constantly struck by the similarities existing in mythic data and ritual practice, even though there might be contrasts in surface nuance. Nevertheless, these contrasts make it difficult to render Aboriginal spiritual belief in any other way than as a vast body of localized myths, Sky Hero identities and individual totemic environments. Yet it is this very diversity that makes Aboriginal belief such a multi-faceted jewel.

But, like the land from which it has sprung, the Dreaming as a viable metaphysic is under threat. Not only has the purity of religious practice as observed by Aborigines in the past all but been destroyed, but the mysteries surrounding those practices have been virtually drained of their numen. European culture, under the burden of its frenetic desire to transform the country into an economic environment, has caused a great deal of damage to what was once a sacralized landscape. Some Aborigines would say that the damage done to their country is irreversible, that the economic and agricultural vandalism of the past two hundred years has made it impossible to redeem their land from its 'fallen' condition.

Few observers would disagree that a great deal of damage has been done in the past. Clearly the Aboriginal social fabric is in tatters. The Rainbow Serpent of the northern waterholes has been dragged from its sanctuaries and allowed to rot on the beach-heads of racial prejudice. The luminous expressions on the Wandjina rock paintings of the Kimberley have been allowed to peel away through indifference. The Aborigines themselves have been allowed, even encouraged, to sink into a morass of self-pity in the hope that they might just 'go away'. In consequence, the Aboriginal 'problem', a problem of continual resistance by an indigenous people to assimilation into the ways of the white man, has consumed countless millions of dollars and caused the growth of vast government bureaucracies throughout the country, all in the hope of ameliorating a race who simply refuse to be pacified in the way that others see fit.

What the Aboriginal people are crying out for and no Government has had the courage to grant them is full title to their tribal lands. This is because economic values in Australia today are a more powerful force than the more fragile, nurturing values of Aboriginal sanctity. No white politician, no agriculturalist, no mining magnate in the current political environment has ever had the courage to stand up and state the subservience of economic aspirations to those of the human spirit. In a world of agnosticism, the idea that spiritual values might correctly hold precedence over the demands of material wellbeing is an unthinkable proposition. Modern man is hell-bent on the destruction of all numinosities, whether they be metaphysical, mythic or totemic, in order that he might pave the way for his own material apotheosis.

This has led to a critical situation among surviving Aborigines. They are at a loss as to how to regain their stolen birthright, except in terms of confrontation and political activism. In turn this has led to a feeling of resentment among European Australians who see Aborigines as opportunists trying to gain for themselves more than their fair share. Aboriginal resentment is quickly dismissed as the whining of urban activists who are 'more white than black'. Accusations of funds mis-use, nepotism, and the sheer waste of federal grants on un-economic enterprises further reduces Aboriginal credibility in the eyes of Europeans. Indeed Aborigines and Aboriginal groups are regarded by many as perpetual mendicants who deserve far less than they're already receiving.

What is the answer to this impasse? If Aboriginal culture is to survive at all, then it requires a far more serious examination of the Dreaming as a metaphysical reality than there has been so far. The Dreaming is at the very root of the Aboriginal heritage, and it is this that must be preserved as a living reality at all costs. Spending money on housing or medical projects, funding artistic communities or economic programmes are extremely important, of course, but must remain as secondary to the re-affirmation of the Dreaming. The Dreaming is the *raison d'etre* of Aboriginal culture. Until this is recognized and acted upon by government and bureaucrats alike, Aborigines will continue to survive in a state of fringe ethnicism, at the mercy of the more dominant European cultural values that surround them.

Recognizing the Dreaming as a living reality, however, demands a fundamental shift in the attitudes of everyone concerned. It requires, firstly, that the Dreaming is seen for what it is: a metaphysical statement about the origins of mankind as a spiritual being. So long as the Dreaming is regarded merely as an assortment of myths that have little more than a quixotic value for the rest of Australians, then the Dreaming will always be demeaned as a metaphysical event. Men and women of goodwill, both European and Aboriginal, must begin to regard the mysteries of the Dreaming as being important in their own lives in the here-and-now. They must begin to see the Dreaming as a spiritual *condition*, rather than simply as a word denoting the creation-time of Aborigines. Indeed the idea that the Dreaming is an on-going metaphysical, rather than an historical event is the only way that this change can be brought about.

In order for this transformation in consciousness to come about, however, it is important that Aborigines regain possession of their totems. To do that, they must have access to their land free from intimidation or interference from governments, mining lobbies and graziers. Regaining possession of their land means that the sanctity of sacred places can be restored and the Dreaming renewed at a ritual level. This resacralization process will inevitably lead to Aboriginal man renewing once more his own commitment to the totemic environment of his forebears. For it is only through the totem that a man makes contact with his Dreaming, and so with the Dreaming of the entire Aboriginal people. If this were to happen, then in the long term the Dreaming might become a sustaining metaphysical principle for all Australians.

This is the lesson that Aborigines can teach everyone. For too long the assumed primitivity of the Aboriginal people has created an environment whereby the relationship between the teacher and those who were being taught favoured Europeans. It has been Europeans who have made judgements and formulated policy about how Aborigines should live and think. It has been Europeans who have studied Aboriginal society under the spell of Darwinian and post-Darwinian evolutionary theories in order to justify European encroachment on their culture — and more particularly, Aboriginal land. And in more recent years, it has been Europeans who have argued against the return of this land to its rightful owners, citing economic detriment as an inevitable result. To support these actions it has been important to maintain the illusion that Aborigines are a 'stone-age' race who are ill-equipped to handle their own lives in the contemporary sphere. That is, in spite of the evidence of 40,000 years of continuous occupation of the country by

Aborigines before the advent of Europeans.

There is no reason why the Dreaming cannot be renewed in the context of contemporary Australian society, in spite of the evidence to the contrary. But it does involve a collective acknowledgement that the land has a sacred dimension rather than a physical one only. Just so long as we are intent on pacifying the landscape and, in a sense, taming it so that its spirit is broken, then we will destroy any hope of the Dreaming as a metaphysical event ever becoming a reality again.

Environments have their own individual genesis, wrote one French writer[1]. This is very true of the Australian continent which has always been the epitome of wildness. It was this wildness that the Aboriginal people sought to preserve in its integrity. They had no desire to pacify their land because they knew that in doing so they would cut off access to its mysteries. A land that remains wild is a land that remains mysterious. Aborigines have always been extremely aware of the power of this mystery, this numen, as a regenerative force for good among men. They know, or have known, that once a land is pacified it loses its power to heal not only itself, but men as well. A land yearns for its freedom just as men do. The Aborigines teach us that by making it a slave to our will, we destroy its ability to challenge us as a friend and colleague.

It is Gregory of Nyssa, one of Christianity's early Church Fathers, who best reflects the Aboriginal's respect for his land. 'What you see on earth and in the heavens, what you behold in the sun and contemplate in the sea, apply this to yourselves and your own nature.' And again: 'As you look upon the universe, see it in your own nature.'[2] Goethe also remarked, 'Man knows himself insofar as he knows the world, becoming aware of it only in himself, and of himself only within it.'[3] Clearly there is a time-honoured tradition demanding of mankind that he equate the integrity of his own nature with that of the land he inhabits. For it is in mutual recognition, mutual acceptance and mutual reverence that the dualities of existence are eliminated, just as the male and female *Churinga* are bound together, or the tiny *Chichurkna* bird wings its way to its double, the *Arumburinga*, at the totem site at death. Spiritual man knows that he cannot survive without due regard for wildness as a reflection of the metaphysical exuberance of earth.

Aborigines who maintain a deep, reverential contact with the Dreaming are true Doctors of the Spirit. It is they who understand the power of land as a principial force and teach us how to respect it. They are true environmentalists who have carried on a tradition of husbandry for countless millennia. For them, true imagination is the power to see subtle processes of nature and their angelic prototypes in the form of spirits of the Dreaming. It is this capacity to reproduce in themselves the 'cosmogenic unfolding,'[4] the permanent creation of the world in the sense in which all creation, finally, is only a Divine Imagination that makes Aborigines so unique. In this sense, they have attained to a state where *summa scientia nihil save* ('The height of knowledge is to know nothing').[5]

The challenge now is to translate this knowledge into some form of action and some form of acknowledgement of the Aboriginal heritage. Granting Land Rights is only an initial step. It does not solve the problem of a renewal of the Dreaming. This can only come about in the form of a commitment to a new level of understanding and respect for Aboriginal traditions and their age-old spirituality. For this to happen, modern man must re-examine his own attitude towards his abhorrence of instinct and the power of the numen as a physical exemplar. He must learn to accept the land on which he lives as an extension to himself, not as a separate entity that should simply be utilized for material gain. He must go beyond what Christopher Bamford calls 'the idea of a single, unique act of creation and assume as well a creative state of continuous and recurrent creation, metaphysical in nature, outside space and time.' When, and if, this happens, we will then begin to see a rebirth of the Dreaming as an extension to our own spirituality.

'When the course of nature goes its proper way, it is a sign that the government is good. But when there is some disturbance in nature there is some error in government.' So said Raphael Pati in his commentary on the Chinese Annals of Confucius, and he was merely affirming what an Aboriginal informant remarked to the author when explaining why Cyclone Tracy devastated the city of Darwin in the Northern Territory sometime in the early 1970s. According to Big Bill Neidjie, the cyclone appeared as a result of the destruction of the Kakadu environment by mining companies, in particular those mining uranium. The cyclone reflected a rupture of chthonic rhythms. As far as he was concerned, the earth around Kakadu had been 'wounded' by this invasion of modern technology bent on absconding with its booty. There had been no ritual requests made of the land prior to commencement of mining, no libations poured on the earth, no corroborees performed to appease the spirit of the earth. It had simply been plundered. In response, Cyclone Tracy did not attack the Kakadu region which was for Aborigines a land still filled with numen, in spite of the presence of mining companies. Instead, the cyclone struck the largest population centre in the North: Darwin. It wreaked havoc at the very centre of urbanism where the spirit of earth had been enchained for some time. If the Territorians had listened to the Confucian injunction, 'The world is a holy vessel. Let him who would tamper with it, beware,' then Cyclone Tracy would never have appeared at all as far as Big Bill was concerned.

Furthermore, there must be an effort made by modern man to accept nomadism as an important human right. It is time to stop thinking of mankind as forever tethered to the one environment, as if 'roots' were the only pre-requisite for existence. Aborigines have long understood the joy of movement about a landscape, just as that other benighted race, the Gypsies. The Oglala Sioux Indian chief, Chief Flying Hawk, best expressed it when he said that 'If the great Spirit wanted men to stay in one place he would make the world stand still. But he made it always change, so birds and animals can move and have green grass and ripe berries, sunlight to work and play in, and night to sleep. Always changing. Everything for good. Nothing for nothing.' A Juki Gypsy of the Lebanon reiterated this point when he remarked 'I say that he should not become absorbed by a single land . . . I wish him a long, long journey over wild wastes and harsh lands, in green places and cool preserves, over islands and unheard-of cities, over the "limits" of this whole age.'[6] Clearly there is a primordial tradition of nomadism unconfined by too strong an association with one place — a tradition that the Aboriginal people have long ago made their own.

Perhaps René Guénon best expressed the dilemma facing the Aborigines and the revival of the Dreaming as a metaphysical principle in our modern age when he wrote:

'Let there be no mistake about it: if the general public accepts the pretext of "civilisation" in all good faith, there are some for whom it amounts to no more than mere economic hypocrisy, a cloak for their designs of conquest and economic civilization; but what strange times indeed, when so many men allow themselves to he persuaded that they are making a people happy by reducing them to subjection, by robbing them of what is most precious in their eyes, namely their own civilization, by compelling them to adopt customs and institutions which were intended for another race, and by coercing them into assuming the most distasteful occupations in order that they may perforce come to acquire things for which they have not the slightest use! That however is the position today: the modern West cannot tolerate the idea that men should prefer to work less and be content to live on little; as quantity alone counts, and as everything that eludes the grasp of the senses is held moreover to be non-existent, it is taken for granted that anyone not producing material things must be an "idler".'[7]

This is precisely the condition under which Aborigines have suffered for two hundred years. They have been subjected to prolonged hardship and human suffering as a colonized people under those who refused to acknowledge any spiritual kinship with them. As a result they have been diminished as a race not only in terms of numbers, but in terms of their own self-esteem. Although attempts are being made now to rectify this situation, very little attempt is being made to acknowledge the Dreaming for what it is. This is because few people understand, or wish to believe in what Giordano Bruno calls the 'diverse spirits and powers'[8] within nature. As long as there is no wish to recognize the divinity in all things, then Aboriginal belief will always be regarded as a suspect philosophy grounded in superstition and strange ritual practices.

These times are precarious in terms of the survival of traditional peoples throughout the world. They are all succumbing like wheat to the blight of modern civilization. It is beholden on us all to arrest this serious devaluation of minorities in the interest of social 'uniformity'. Numbarkala, Wandjina, the Rainbow Serpent, Ungud — whatever name the presiding spirit of the Dreaming goes under — they are all but a manifestation of man's need to maintain vigilance against the threat of spiritual extinction. It is not traditional man that will die out when the last Aborigine or Sioux or Kalahari Bushman quits this earth; it will be the spirit of man as nature's consort that will finally disappear. This alone is worth fighting for, not the economic hegemonies or industrial wastelands that now threaten to blight this earth.

The Dreaming still exists. The pure asceticism of nature as an attainable condition within every one of us is possible if we listen to what the Aborigine is saying to us. Re-establishing our links with totems, making our own Dream Journeys, listening to the voice of our own Dreaming and acknowledging our ancestors as being primordially present, is the beginning of the process of renewal. When this is achieved, then the revival of the Dreaming as a metaphysical condition will be a reality. Then we will be able to say, along with Big Bill Neidjie, 'Dreaming place . . . you can't change it, no matter who you are. No matter you rich man, no matter you king. You can't change it.' Indeed, it is this very unchangeability of the Dreaming that makes it so steadfast in the lives of all Aborigines — and us if we wish it to be so.

Notes

1. *Nature Word*. R.A. Schwaller de Lubicz, Lindesfarne Press.

2. *The Cycle of Desire*. Commentary on Ecclesiastes, homily 1. St Gregory of Nyssa.

3. *Botanical Writings*. Goethe.

4. See Maurice Aniane's *Material for Thought* for a more detailed analysis of this remarkable concept.

5. Christian Rosen Kreutz.

6. *The World of the Juki*. Douglas Halebi, Studies in Comparative Religion, 1983.

7. *The Crisis of the Modern World*, René Guénon, Luzac.

8. Cf. 'For . . . diverse living things represent spirits and powers, which beyond the absolute being which they have, obtain a being communicated to all things according to their capacity and measure . . . thus one should think of Sol (Sun) as being in a crocus, a daffodil, a sunflower, in the cock, in the lion . . . For as the divinity descends to a certain measure in as such as it communicates itself to nature, so there is an ascent made to the divinity through nature.' Giordano Bruno, *Spaccio dellabastia trionforte*. Dialogue 3.

Select Bibliography

Aniane, Maurice. *Material for Thought*. Spring Books. 1976.

Berndt, R.M. & C.H.. *The World of the First Aborigines*. Ure Smith. 1976.

Berndt, R.M. *Three Faces of Love*. Nelson. 1976.

Beveridge, P. *The Aborigines of Victoria and the Riverina*. 1889.

Budge, Wallis. *The Book of Paradise 1-11*. London 1904.

Brain, Robert. *The Decorated Body*. Harper & Row. 1979.

The Bhagavad Gita. Penguin Classics. 1982.

Campbell, J. *The Mysteries*. (edit.) Bollingen Series XXX. 1978.

Collins, David. *An Account of an English Colony in N.S.W.*

Corbin, Henry. *Spiritual Body and Celestial Earth*. Bollingen series XCI. 2. 1977.

Elkin, A.P. *Aboriginal Men of High Degree*. University of Queensland Press. 1977.

Elkin, A.P. *The Australian Aborigines*. Angus and Robertson. 1974.

Eliade, Mircea. *The Two and the One*. Harvil Press. 1965.

Eliade, Mircea. *Myths, Dreams and Memories*. Fontana Library 1968.

Fraser, J.G. *The Golden Bough*. The Macmillan Press. 1978.

Griaule, Marcel. *Conversations with Ogotommeli*. Oxford University Press. 1980.

Guénon, René. *The Lord of the World*. Combe Spring Press. 1983.

Guénon, René. *Crisis of the Modern World*. Luzac. 1975.

Graves, Robert. *The White Goddess*. Faber & Faber. 1977.

Jung, C.G. *Symbols of Transformation*. Routledge Kegan Paul. 1965

Jung, C.G. *Alchemical Studies*. Routledge Kegan Paul. 1967.

Kerényi, C. *The Gods of the Greeks*. Thames and Hudson. 1974.

Mountford, C.P. *Ayres Rock: its People, their Beliefs and their Art*. Pacific Books. 1971.

Mountford, C.P. *Winbaraku and the Myth of Jarapiri*. Rigby. 1968.

Malory, Sir Thomas. *Le Mort d'Arthur*. Penguin Books. 1969.

Montagu, Ashley. *Coming into Being among Australian Aborigines*. Routledge Kegan Paul. 1974.

Mohammed. *The Koran*. Oxford Paperbacks. 1985.

Neihardt, John. *Black Elk Speaks*. Pocket Books 1975.

Neidjie, Big Bill. *Kakadu Man*. Resource Managers, Darwin. 1988.

Otto, Walter. *The Homeric Gods*. Thames and Hudson. 1979.

Parker, K.L. *More Australian Legendary Tales*. 1898.

Pound, Ezra. *The Cantos*. Faber & Faber. 1975.

Plotinus. *The Enneads*. Tr. Stephen Mackenna. Faber & Faber. 1969.

Proclus. *Treatise on the Hieratic Arts of the Greeks*.

Rilke, R.M. *The Duino Elegies*. The Hogarth Press. 1975,

The Rig Veda. Penguin Classics. 1981.

Rossbach, Sarah. *Feng Shui. The Chinese Art of Placement*. E.P. Dutton. 1983.

Sivin, Nathan. *Chinese Alchemy: Preliminary Studies*. Harvard University Press. 1968.

Strehlow, T.G. *The Arunta Traditions*. Melbourne University Press 1947.

Spencer & Gillen. *Native Tribes of Australia*. 1899.

Stanner, W.E.H. *White Man Got No Dreaming*. ANU Press. 1979.

Suhrawardi, Shihabuddin Yahya. *Oeuvres philosophiques et mystiques de Sohrawardi*. Opera metaphysica et mystica. Teheran and Paris. 1952.

Schwaller de Lubicz, R. *Nature Word*. Lindesfarne Press. 1982.

Schwaller de Lubicz, R. *Symbol and Symbolic*. Inner Traditions. 1978.

The Upanishads. Penguin Classics. 1981.

Zimmer, Heinrich. *The Kingdom and the Corpse*. Meridian Books. 1960.

Index